HANDS-ON HISTORY!
ANCIENT CHINA

STEP INTO THE TIME OF THE CHINESE EMPIRE, WITH 15 STEP-BY-STEP
PROJECTS AND OVER 300 EXCITING PICTURES   **PHILIP STEELE**
CONSULTANT: JESSIE LIM

ARMADILLO

This edition is published by Armadillo,
an imprint of Anness Publishing Ltd, Blaby Road,
Wigston, Leicestershire LE18 4SE; info@anness.com

www.annesspublishing.com

If you like the images in this book and would like to investigate
using them for publishing, promotions or advertising, please
visit www.practicalpictures.com for more information.

Publisher: Joanna Lorenz
Managing Editor, Children's Books: Sue Grabham
Senior Editor: Neil Kelly
Project Editor: Sophie Warne
Editor: Charlotte Hurdman
Readers: Felicity Forster, Joy Wotton
Designers: Matthew Cook, Alison Walker
Illustration: Robert Ashby, Stuart Carter, Shane Marsh
Photography: John Freeman
Stylist: Konica Shankar
Additional Styling: Melanie Williams
Production Controller: Ann Childers

PICTURE CREDITS
b=bottom, t=top, m=middle, l=left, r=right
Ancient Art and Architecture Collection Ltd: pages 15br, 56tl,
58ml; Bridgeman Art Library: pages 15tl, 16ml, 21tr, 23br,
25bl, 31tl, 31ml, 33bl, 41bl, 45tl, 46ml, 47ml, 47mr; Bruce
Coleman: pages 25br, 39tl; James Davis Worldwide
Photographic Travel Library: pages 5tr, 17ml, 36br; C M
Dixon: pages 12tl, 14bl, 24tl, 30tr, 43tl, 44tr; E T Archive:
pages 8l, 9tl, 9tr, 9bl, 11t, 11bl, 12bl, 15tr, 15bl, 17tr, 20br,
21br, 22tr, 22bl, 23bl, 24br, 25tr, 26tr, 27tr, 32bl, 40br, 43tr,
47tl, 49ml, 50mr, 54bl, 57ml, 61t; Mary Evans Picture
Library: pages 11br, 12br, 22br, 29tl, 42br, 59tl; FLPA: pages
43mr, 43br; Werner Forman Archive: pages 10bl, 13tr, 26mr,
29tr, 29ml, 38tr, 39bl, 39br, 40bl, 44ml, 48m, 50tl, 51ml,
55tr, 59tr; Michael Holford: pages 4tl, 35tr, 36tr, 37br, 42tl,
58tr; The Hutchinson Library: pages 52ml, 60m, 61ml;
MacQuitty Collection: pages 5m, 20tr, 21bl, 25tl, 27ml, 32tr,
37b, 41br, 43bl, 45tr, 46tl, 48tr, 53tl, 53tr, 53ml, 54tl, 55ml,
55br, 59ml; Papilio Photographic: page 30ml; TRIP: pages
10br, 60tr; Visual Arts Library: pages 8r, 9br, 14tl, 14m, 20bl,
23tr, 28ml, 34tl, 35ml, 40tl, 41bl, 41tr, 44mr, 49tl, 51tl, 51tr,
55tl, 56ml; ZEFA: pages 4m, 10tr, 13tl, 13b, 16tl, 18tr, 33tr,
33br, 36tl, 37tl, 37tr, 38tl, 39tr, 47tr.

Manufacturer: Anness Publishing Ltd, Blaby Road, Wigston,
Leicestershire LE18 4SE, England
For Product Tracking go to:
www.annesspublishing.com/tracking
Batch: 0948-21490-1127

CONTENTS

Anness Publishing would like to thank the
following children for appearing in this
book: Lucilla Braune, Aileen Greiner,
Francesca Hill, Alex Lindblom-Smith,
Sophie Lindblom-Smith, Daniel Ofori,
Vanessa Ofori, Edward Parker, Claudia
Martins Silva, Clleon Smith, Nicky Stafford,
Saif Uddowlla, Kirsty Wells. Gratitude also
to their parents, and to Hampden Gurney
and Walnut Tree Walk Schools.

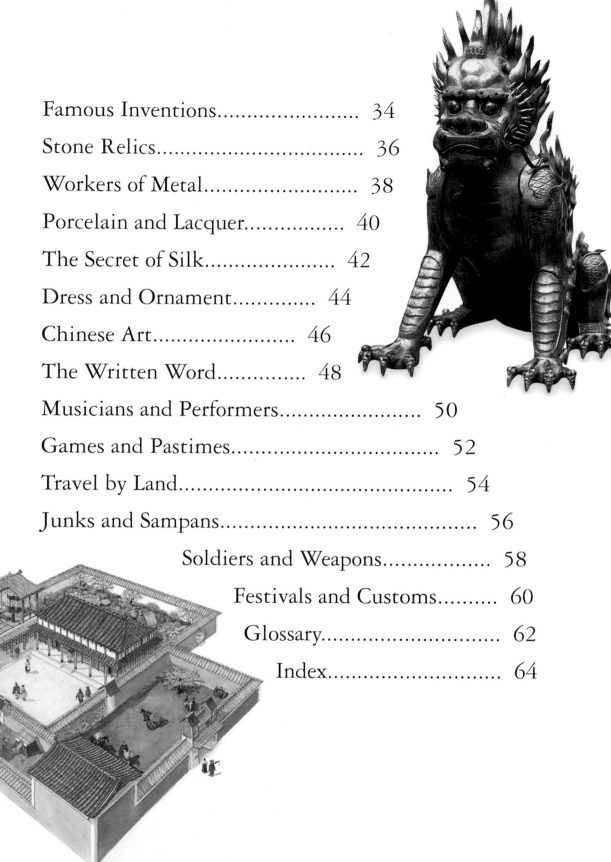

An Ancient Civilization

IMAGINE YOU COULD travel back in time 5,000 years and visit the lands of the Far East. In northern China you would come across smoky settlements of small thatched huts. You might see villagers fishing in rivers, sowing millet or baking pottery. From these small beginnings, China developed into an amazing civilization. Its towns grew into huge cities, with palaces and temples. Many Chinese became great writers, thinkers, artists, builders and inventors. China was first united under the rule of a single emperor in 221BC, and continued to be ruled by emperors until 1912.

China today is a modern country. Its ancient past has to be pieced together by archaeologists and historians. They dig up ancient tombs and settlements, and study textiles, ancient books and pottery. Their job is made easier because historical records were kept. These provide much information about the long history of Chinese civilization.

REST IN PEACE
A demon is trodden into defeat by a guardian spirit. Statues like this were commonly put in tombs to protect the dead against evil spirits.

ALL THE EMPEROR'S MEN
A vast model army marches again. It was dug up by archaeologists in 1974, and is now on display near Xian. The lifesize figures are made of terracotta (baked clay). They were buried in 210BC near the tomb of Qin Shi Huangdi, the first emperor of all China. He believed that they would protect him from evil spirits after he died.

TIMELINE 7000BC–110BC

Prehistoric remains of human ancestors dating back to 600,000BC have been found in China's Shaanxi province. The beginnings of Chinese civilization may be seen in the farming villages of the late Stone Age (8000BC–2500BC). As organized states grew up, the Chinese became skilled at warfare, working metals and making elaborate pottery and fine silk.

Banpo hut

*c.*7000BC Bands of hunters and fishers roam freely around the river valleys of China. They use simple stone tools and weapons.

*c.*3200BC Farming villages such as Banpo produce pottery in kilns. This way of life is called the Yangshao culture.

*c.*2100BC The start of a legendary 500-year period of rule, known as the XIA DYNASTY.

*c.*2000BC Black pottery is made by the people of the so-called Longshan culture.

Shang bronze vessel

*c.*1600BC Beginning of the SHANG DYNASTY. Bronze worked and silk produced. The first picture-writing is used (on bones for telling fortunes).

1122BC Zhou ruler Wu defeats Shang emperor. Wu becomes emperor of the WESTERN ZHOU DYNASTY.

Zhou spearheads

7000BC   2100BC   1600BC

THE HAN EMPIRE (206BC–AD220)

China grew rapidly during the Han dynasty. By AD2 it had expanded to take in North Korea, the southeast coast, the southwest as far as Vietnam and large areas of Central Asia. Northern borders were defended by the Great Wall, which was extended during Han rule.

A HEAVENLY HALL

The Hall of Prayer for Good Harvests (*shown right*) is part of Tiantan, the Temple of Heavenly Peace in Beijing. It was originally built in 1420, but had to be rebuilt in the 1890s after it was destroyed by lightning. Buildings like these tell us about traditional technology and design, as well as about Chinese religious beliefs.

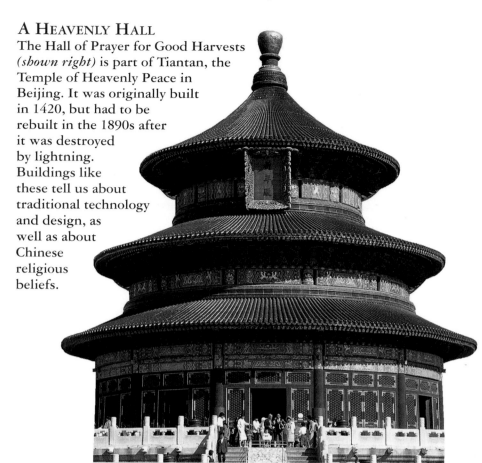

THE JADE PRINCE

In 1968, Chinese archaeologists excavated the tomb of Prince Liu Sheng. His remains were encased in a jade suit when he died in about 100BC. Over 2,400 pieces of this precious stone were joined with gold wire. It was believed that jade would preserve the body.

Zhou soldier

771BC Capital city moves from Anyang to Luoyang. Beginning of EASTERN ZHOU DYNASTY.

*c.*604BC Birth of the legendary Laozi, founder of Daoism.

551BC Teacher and philosopher Kong Fuzi (Confucius) born.

513BC Iron-working develops.

453BC Break-up of central rule. Small states fight each other for 200 years. Work begins on Grand Canal and Great Wall.

221BC China unites as a centralized empire under Zheng (Qin Shi Huangdi). Great Wall is extended.

213BC Qin Shi Huangdi burns all books that are not 'practical'.

Chinese writing

210BC Death of Qin Shi Huangdi. Terracotta army guards his tomb, near Chang'an (modern Xian).

206BC QIN DYNASTY overthrown. Beginnings of HAN DYNASTY as Xiang Yu and Liu Bang fight for control of the Han kingdom.

202BC The WESTERN HAN DYNASTY formally begins. It is led by the former official Liu Bang, who becomes emperor Gaozu.

200BC Chang'an becomes the capital city of the Chinese empire.

terracotta warrior and horse

112BC Trade with the peoples of Western Asia and Europe begins to flourish along the Silk Road.

780BC   550BC   210BC   140BC   110BC

The Middle Kingdom

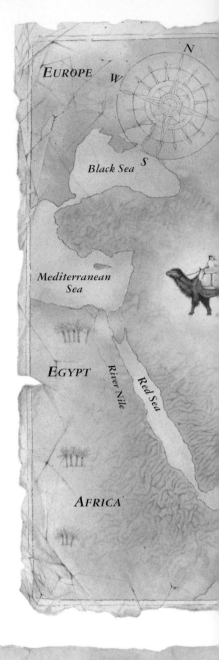

CHINA IS A VAST COUNTRY, about the size of Europe. Its fertile plains and river valleys are ringed by many deserts, mountains and oceans. The ancient Chinese named their land Zhongguo, the Middle Kingdom, and believed that it was at the centre of the civilized world. Most Chinese belong to a people called the Han, but the country is also inhabited by 50 or more different peoples, some of whom have played an important part in Chinese history. These groups include the Hui, Zhuang, Dai, Yao, Miao, Tibetans, Manchus and Mongols.

The very first Chinese civilizations grew up around the Huang He (Yellow River), where the fertile soil supported farming villages and then towns and cities. These became the centres of rival kingdoms. Between 1700 and 256BC Chinese rule spread southwards to the Chang Jiang (Yangzi River), the great river of Central China. All of eastern China was united within a single empire for the first time during Qin rule (221–206BC).

The rulers of the Han dynasty (206BC–AD220) then expanded the empire southwards as far as Vietnam. The Chinese empire was now even larger than the Roman empire, dominating Central and South-east Asia. The Mongols, from lands to the north of China, ruled the empire from 1279 to 1368. They were succeeded by the Ming dynasty, which was in turn overthown by the Manchu in 1644. In later centuries, China became inward-looking and unable to resist interference from Europe. The empire finally collapsed, with China declaring itself a republic in 1912.

TIMELINE 110BC–AD960

AD9 The Western Han dynasty is challenged by Wang Mang.

AD25 The EASTERN HAN DYNASTY begins under Liu Xiu, after a peasant uprising. Its capital is at Luoyang.

city of Luoyang

c.AD26–225 Trade increases and a civil service is established. The first national library is built. Paper is invented, and an accurate calendar developed.

book printed on bamboo

AD65–100 The Buddhist religion takes root in China.

AD184 A peasant revolution called the Yellow Turban Rebellion takes place against Han dynasty rule.

AD220–280 Break-up of empire into separate kingdoms and dynasties. Cultural influence from India reaches China.

AD440 Daoism becomes official religion in north. Advances in mathematics and technology.

AD490 Longmen caves carved with Buddhist images.

AD581 SUI DYNASTY begins.

AD585 Main work on Grand Canal linking Chang Jiang with Huang He. Extension of Great Wall.

Tao Yuanmin, Chinese poet c.AD300s

AD618 Beginning of the TANG DYNASTY.

AD630–658 Chinese power and influence extends to cover Kashmir, Afghanistan and the river Oxus.

110BC   AD26   AD200   AD590

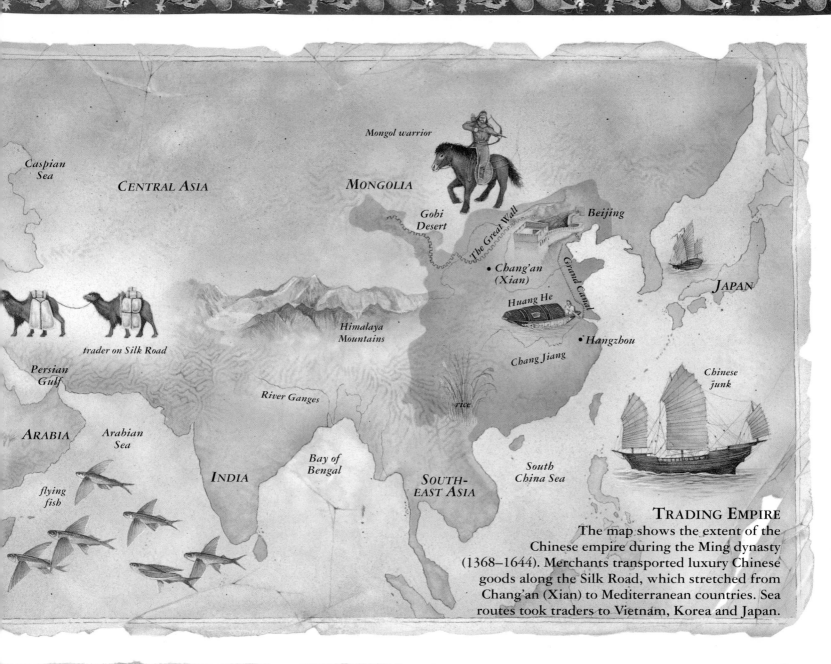

Caspian Sea

CENTRAL ASIA

MONGOLIA

Mongol warrior

Gobi Desert

The Great Wall

Beijing

Chang'an (Xian)

Grand Canal

JAPAN

Huang He

Hangzhou

Chang Jiang

rice

Chinese junk

trader on Silk Road

Persian Gulf

Himalaya Mountains

ARABIA

Arabian Sea

River Ganges

Bay of Bengal

INDIA

SOUTH-EAST ASIA

South China Sea

flying fish

TRADING EMPIRE

The map shows the extent of the Chinese empire during the Ming dynasty (1368–1644). Merchants transported luxury Chinese goods along the Silk Road, which stretched from Chang'an (Xian) to Mediterranean countries. Sea routes took traders to Vietnam, Korea and Japan.

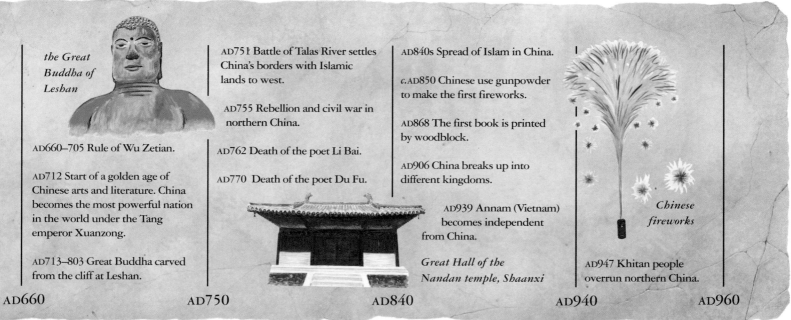

the Great Buddha of Leshan

AD660–705 Rule of Wu Zetian.

AD712 Start of a golden age of Chinese arts and literature. China becomes the most powerful nation in the world under the Tang emperor Xuanzong.

AD713–803 Great Buddha carved from the cliff at Leshan.

AD751 Battle of Talas River settles China's borders with Islamic lands to west.

AD755 Rebellion and civil war in northern China.

AD762 Death of the poet Li Bai.

AD770 Death of the poet Du Fu.

Great Hall of the Nandan temple, Shaanxi

AD840s Spread of Islam in China.

*c.*AD850 Chinese use gunpowder to make the first fireworks.

AD868 The first book is printed by woodblock.

AD906 China breaks up into different kingdoms.

AD939 Annam (Vietnam) becomes independent from China.

Chinese fireworks

AD947 Khitan people overrun northern China.

AD660   AD750   AD840   AD940   AD960

Makers of History

GREAT EMPIRES ARE made by ordinary people as much as by their rulers. The Chinese empire could not have been built without the millions of peasants who planted crops, built defensive walls and dug canals. The names of these people are largely forgotten, except for those who led uprisings and revolts against their rulers. The inventors, thinkers, artists, poets and writers of imperial China are better known. They had a great effect on the society they lived in, and left behind ideas, works of art and inventions that still influence people today.

The royal court was made up of thousands of officials, artists, craftsmen and servants. Some had great political power. China's rulers came from many different backgrounds and peoples.

Many emperors were ruthless former warlords who were hungry for power. Others are remembered as scholars or artists. Some women also achieved great political influence, openly or from behind the scenes.

LAOZI (born *c.*604BC)
The legendary Laozi is said to have been a scholar who worked as a court librarian. It is thought that he wrote the book known as the *Daodejing*. He believed people should live in harmony with nature, and his ideas later formed the basis of Daoism.

KONG FUZI (551–479BC)
Kong Fuzi is better known in the West by the Latin version of his name, Confucius. He was a public official who became an influential teacher and thinker. His views on family life, society, and the treatment of others greatly influenced later generations.

TIMELINE AD960–1912

Kublai Khan

AD960 The SONG DYNASTY begins.

1040 The Chinese invent a new method of printing that uses movable blocks of type.

1100 Further work is carried out on the Grand Canal.

1215–1223 Mongols led by Genghis Khan invade the north of China.

1260 Kublai Khan, son of the feared Mongol warrior and ruler Genghis Khan, becomes the Mongol emperor.

1275 Marco Polo said to have reached the Mongol capital of Khanbalik (Beijing).

printed paper money

1279 Mongols invade and conquer southern China, ending the Song reign. YUAN DYNASTY begins.

1340s Moroccan explorer Ibn Batuta visits China.

1349 Chinese settle at Singapore.

1351 Red Turban Rebellion against Mongol rule.

1363 Zhu Yuanzhang leads a fierce rebellion.

Zheng He's rudder

1368 Zhu Yuanzhang becomes emperor. Start of MING DYNASTY, with the capital at Nanjing.

1403–1435 Work on Great Wall.

AD960   AD1200   AD1278   AD1365

QIN SHI HUANGDI (256–210BC)
Scholars plead for their lives before the first emperor. Zheng came to the throne of a state called Qin at the age of nine. He went on to rule all China and was given his full title, meaning First Emperor of Qin. His brutal methods included burying his opponents alive.

HAN GAOZU (256–195BC)
In the Qin dynasty (221–206BC) Liu Bang was a minor public official in charge of a relay station for royal messengers. He watched as the centralized Qin empire fell apart. In 206BC he declared himself ruler of the Han kingdom. In 202BC he defeated his opponent, Xiang Yu, and founded the Han dynasty. As emperor Gaozu, he tried to unite China without using Qin's harsh methods.

EMPRESS WU ZETIAN
(AD624–705)
The emperor Tang Gaozong enraged officials when he replaced his legal wife with Wu, his concubine (secondary wife). After the emperor suffered a stroke in AD660, Wu took control of the country. In AD690 she became the only woman in history to declare herself empress of China.

KUBLAI KHAN (AD1214–1294)
The Venetian explorer Marco Polo visits emperor Kublai Khan at Khanbalik (Beijing). Kublai Khan was a Mongol who conquered northern, and later southern, China.

1405–33 Chinese voyages of exploration under Zheng He.

1421 Beijing becomes the capital city of the Chinese empire.

Manchu warrior

1428 The Chinese are expelled from Annam (Vietnam).

1550 Japanese pirates mount raids on China. Mongols invade north again.

1644 Li Zicheng leads a rebellion against Ming rule. Manchu invasion. QING DYNASTY founded.

Boxer rebels

1673 Rebellions against Qing rule in south.

1839–42 First Opium War as Britain forces China to accept opium imports from India.

1842 Treaty of Nanjing. Britain gains Hong Kong.

1850–64 Taiping rebellion.

1858 Treaty of Tianjin. Chinese ports taken over by foreign powers.

1862 The Empress Dowager Cixi becomes regent.

1894–95 War with Japan. Loss of Taiwan.

1899–1900 Boxer Rebellion against Qing and foreign governments.

1908 Last emperor, Puyi, ascends to throne as a small boy.

1912 Declaration of republic by Sun Yatsen. Emperor Puyi abdicates.

Puyi, the last emperor

AD1405   AD1425   AD1650   AD1880   AD1912

The Sons of Heaven

THE FIRST CHINESE RULERS lived about 4,000 years ago. This early dynasty (period of rule) was known as the Xia. We know little about the Xia rulers, because this period of Chinese history has become mixed up with ancient myths and legends. Excavations have told us more about the Shang dynasty rulers of over 3,000 years ago, who were waited on by slaves and had fabulous treasures.

During the next period of rule, the Zhou dynasty, an idea grew up that the Chinese rulers were Sons of Heaven, placed on the throne by the will of the gods. After China became a powerful, united empire in 221BC, this idea helped keep the emperors in power. Rule of the empire was passed down from father to son. Anyone who seized the throne by force had to show that the overthrown ruler had offended the gods. Earthquakes and natural disasters were often taken as signs of the gods' displeasure.

Chinese emperors were among the most powerful rulers in history. Emperors of China's last dynasty, the Qing (1644–1912), lived in luxurious palaces that were cut off from the world. When they travelled through the streets, the common people had to stay indoors.

WHERE EMPERORS PRAYED
These beautifully decorated pillars can be seen inside the Hall of Prayer for Good Harvests at Tiantan in Beijing. An emperor was a religious leader as well as a political ruler, and would arrive here in a great procession each New Year. The evening would be spent praying to the gods for a plentiful harvest in the coming year.

TO THE HOLY MOUNTAIN
This stele (inscribed stone) is located on the summit of China's holiest mountain, Taishan, in Shandong province. To the ancient Chinese, Taishan was the home of the gods. For over 2,000 years the emperors climbed the carved steps to the temple to offer prayers.

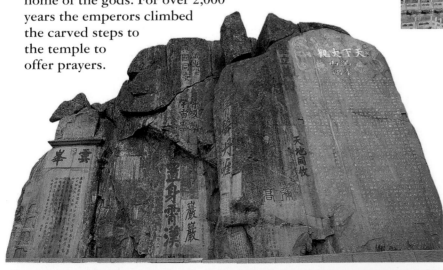

IN THE FORBIDDEN CITY
The vast Imperial Palace in Beijing is best described as 'a city within a city'. It was built between 1407 and 1420 by hundreds of thousands of labourers under the command of Emperor Yongle. Behind its high, red walls and moats were 800 beautiful halls and temples, set amongst gardens, courtyards and bridges. No fewer than 24 emperors lived here in incredible luxury, set apart from their subjects. The Imperial Palace was also known as the Forbidden City, as ordinary Chinese people were not even allowed to approach its gates.

"WE POSSESS ALL THINGS"

This was the message sent from Emperor Qianlong to the British King George III in 1793. Here the emperor is being presented with a gift of fine horses from the Kyrgyz people of Central Asia. By the late 1800s, Chinese rule took in Mongolia, Tibet and Central Asia. All kinds of fabulous gifts were sent to the emperor from every corner of the empire, as everyone wanted to win his favour.

RITUALS AND CEREMONIES

During the Qing dynasty, an emperor's duties included many long ceremonies and official receptions. Here in Beijing's Forbidden City, a long carpet leads to the ruler's throne. Officials in silk robes line the steps and terraces, holding their banners and ceremonial umbrellas high. Courtiers kneel and bow before the emperor. Behaviour at the royal court was set out in the greatest detail. Rules decreed which kind of clothes could be worn and in which colours.

CARRIED BY HAND

The first Chinese emperor, Qin Shi Huangdi, is carried to a monastery high in the mountains in the 200s BC. He rides in a litter (a type of chair) that is carried on his servants' shoulders. Emperors always travelled with a large following of guards and courtiers.

Religions and Beliefs

"THREE TEACHINGS FLOW INTO ONE" is an old saying in China. The three teachings are Daoism, Confucianism and Buddhism. In China they gradually mingled together over the ages.

The first Chinese peoples believed in various gods and goddesses of nature, in spirits and demons. The spirit of nature and the flow of life inspired the writings which are said to be the work of Laozi (born *c.*604BC). His ideas formed the basis of the Daoist religion.

The teachings of Kong Fuzi (Confucius) come from the same period of history but they stress the importance of social order and respect for ancestors as a source of happiness. At this time another great religious teacher, the Buddha, was preaching in India. Within 500 years Buddhist teachings had reached China, and by the Tang dynasty (AD618–906) Buddhism was the most popular religion. Islam arrived at this time and won followers in the northwest. Christianity also came into China from Persia, but few Chinese were converted to this religion until the 1900s.

THE MERCIFUL GODDESS
Guanyin was the goddess of mercy and the bringer of children. She was a holy figure for all Chinese Buddhists.

DAOISM – A RELIGION OF HARMONY
A young boy is taught the Daoist belief in the harmony of nature. Daoists believe that the natural world is in a state of balance between two forces – yin and yang. Yin is dark, cool and feminine, while yang is light, hot and masculine. The two forces are combined in the black and white symbol on the scroll.

PEACE THROUGH SOCIAL ORDER
Kong Fuzi (Confucius) looks out on to an ordered world. He taught that the well-being of society depends on duty and respect. Children should obey their parents and wives should obey their husbands. The people should obey their rulers, and rulers should respect the gods. All of the emperors followed the teachings of Confucianism.

ISLAM IN CHINA
This is part of the Great Mosque in Xian (ancient Chang'an), built in the Chinese style. The mosque was founded in AD742, but most of the buildings in use today date from the Ming dynasty (1368–1644). Islam first took root in China in about AD700. Moslem traders from Central Asia brought with them the Koran, the holy book of Islam. It teaches that there is only one god, Allah, and that Muhammad is his prophet.

FREEDOM FROM DESIRE
Chinese monks carved huge statues of the Buddha from rock. Some can be seen at the Mogao caves near Dunhuang, where temples were built as early as AD366. The Buddha taught that suffering is caused by our love of material things. Buddhists believe that we are born over and over again until we learn to conquer this desire.

TEMPLE GUARDIANS
Gilded statues of Buddhist saints ward off evil spirits at Puningsi, the Temple of Universal Peace, near Chengde. The temple was built in 1755 in the Tibetan style. It is famed for its Mahayana Hall, a tower roofed in gilded bronze.

Chinese Society

THE RIVER VALLEYS AND COASTS of China have always been among the most crowded places on Earth. Confucius, with his love of social order, had taught that this vast society could be divided into four main groups. At the top were the nobles, the scholars and the landowners. Next came the farmers, including even the poorest peasants. These people were valued because they worked for the good of the whole nation, providing the vast amounts of food necessary to feed an ever-increasing population. In third place were skilled workers and craftsmen. In the lowest place of all were the merchants, because Confucius believed they worked for their own profit rather than for the good of the people as a whole. However, the way in which Chinese society rewarded these groups in practice did not fit the theory at all. Merchants ended up becoming the richest citizens, lending money to the upper classes. In contrast, the highly valued peasants often led a wretched life, losing their homes to floods and earthquakes or starving in years of famine.

TOP BRASS
This is what important government officials would have looked like in the early 1600s. The government employed several thousand high-ranking officials. The civil service was regarded as the most honourable and best rewarded profession. The entry examinations were open to all men. Even the poor could rise to ruling class if they passed the examinations.

THE IDEAL ORDER?
A government official tours the fields, where respectful peasants are happily at work. This painting shows an idealized view of the society proposed by Confucius. The district prospers and flourishes because everybody knows their place in society. The reality was very different – while Chinese officials led comfortable lives, most people were very poor and suffered great hardship. They toiled in the fields for little reward. Officials provided aid for the victims of famine or flood, but they never tackled the injustice of the social order. Peasant uprisings were common through much of Chinese history.

WORKING IN THE CLAYPITS

The manufacture of pottery was one of imperial China's most important industries. There were state-owned factories as well as many smaller private workshops. The industry employed some very highly skilled workers, and also thousands of unskilled labourers whose job was to dig out the precious clay. They had to work very hard for little pay. Sometimes there were serious riots to demand better working conditions.

DRAGON-BACKBONE MACHINE

Peasants enlist the aid of machinery to help work the rice fields. The life of a peasant was mostly made up of back-breaking toil. The relentless work was made slightly easier by some clever, labour-saving inventions. The square-pallet chain pump (*shown above*) was invented in about AD100. It was known as the dragon-backbone machine and was used to raise water to the flooded terraces where rice was grown. Men and women worked from dawn to dusk to supply food for the population.

LIFE BEHIND A DESK

Country magistrates try to remember the works of Confucius during a tough public examination. A pass would provide them with a path to wealth and social success. A failure would mean disgrace. The Chinese civil service was founded in about 900BC. This painting dates from the Qing dynasty (1644–1912). There were exams for all ranks of officials and they were very hard. The classic writings had to be remembered by heart. Not surprisingly, candidates sometimes cheated!

TOKENS OF WEALTH

Merchants may have had low social status, but they had riches beyond the dreams of peasants. They amassed wealth through money-lending and by exporting luxury goods, such as silk, spices and tea. The influence of the merchant class is reflected in the first bronze Chinese coins (*c*.250BC), which were shaped to look like knives, hoes and spades. Merchants commonly traded or bartered in these tools.

knife

hoe

Towns and Cities

CITIES GREW UP in northern China during the Shang dynasty (*c*.1600–1122BC). Zhengzhou was one of the first capitals, built in about 1600BC. Its city wall was 7km/4 miles long, but the city spilled out far beyond this border. Chinese cities increased in size over the centuries, and by the AD1500s the city of Beijing was the biggest in the world. Some great cities became centres of government, while smaller settlements served as market towns or manufacturing centres.

A typical Chinese city was surrounded by a wide moat and a high wall of packed earth. It was entered through a massive gatehouse set into the wall. The streets were filled with carts, beggars, craft workshops and street markets. Most people lived in small districts called wards that were closed off at night by locked gates. Temples and monasteries were a common sight, but royal palaces and the homes of rich families were hidden by high walls.

THE SOUND OF BELLS
Bells were set up at temples and also on towers in the cities. They were struck at daybreak to mark the opening of the gates. Big drums were struck when they were closed at night.

CHINESE SKYSCRAPERS
A pagoda (*shown far left*) soars above the skyline of a town in imperial China. Pagodas were graceful towers up to 15 floors high, with eaves projecting at each level. Buildings rather like these were first seen in India, where they often marked holy Buddhist sites. The Chinese perfected the design, and many people believed that building pagodas spread good fortune over the surrounding land. Sometimes they were used as libraries, where scholars would study Buddhist scriptures.

MAKE A PAGODA
You will need: cardboard, ruler, pencil, scissors, glue and brush, masking tape, corrugated card, 3 x 1.5cm/1¼ x ¾in diameter dowel, embroidery bobbin, half a wooden skewer, paint (pink, terracotta and cream), thick and thin paintbrushes, water pot.

Roof: level 1 — 35cm/14in × 35cm/14in

Side: level 1 (x 4) — 30cm/12in × 11.5cm/4½in
Doorway 4cm/1½in × 8cm/3¼in

Spire sides (x 4) — 2.5cm/1in, 4.5cm/1¾in, 7cm/2¾in

(NB The doorway is 4 x 8cm/ 1½ x 3in for all levels)

Roof: levels 2–7
Level 2 32 x 32cm/12¾ x 12¾in
Level 3 29 x 29cm/11½ x 11½in
Level 4 26 x 26cm/10½ x 10½in
Level 5 23 x 23cm/9 x 9in
Level 6 20 x 20cm/8 x 8in
Level 7 17 x 17cm/6½ x 6½in

Side (x 4): levels 2–7
Level 2 27 x 11.5cm/10½ x 4½in
Level 3 24 x 11.5cm/9½ x 4½in
Level 4 21 x 11.5cm/8½ x 4½in
Level 5 18 x 11.5cm/7 x 4½in
Level 6 15 x 11.5cm/6 x 4½in
Level 7 12 x 11.5cm/4½ x 4½in

Cut out roof, side and spire pieces from thick cardboard. Use the measurements shown above (pieces not to scale).

1 Start with level 1. Glue four side pieces together. Hold together with masking tape. Then glue pieces of card behind each doorway.

Lower Class ward

Middle Class ward

Upper Class ward

Government buildings

Markets

Offices

Palace

CITY PLANNING

This grid shows the layout of Chang'an (Xian), the capital city of the empire during the Tang dynasty (AD618–906). The streets were grouped into small areas called wards. The design of many Chinese cities followed a similar pattern.

WESTERN INFLUENCE

The flags of Western nations fly in the great southern port of Guangzhou (Canton) in about 1810. Foreign architectural styles also began to appear in some Chinese cities at this time. In the early 1800s, powerful Western countries competed to take over Chinese trade and force their policies upon the emperor.

LIVING ON THE RIM

Cities around the edge of the empire were unlike those of typical Chinese towns. The mountain city of Lhasa is the capital of Tibet. It stretches out below its towering palace, the Potala. Tibet has had close political links with China since the AD600s. The country did remain independent for most of its history, but was invaded by China in the 1700s and again in 1950.

Pagodas were built in China as early as AD523. Some of the first ones were built by Chinese monks who had seen Buddhist holy temples in India. Extra floors were sometimes added on over the centuries.

2 Glue level 1 roof on top of level 1 walls. Allow to dry. Centre level 2 sides on roof below. Glue down and hold with tape. Add level 2 roof.

3 Cut four 3cm/1¼in-wide corrugated card strips for each roof. The lengths need to match the roof measurements. Glue to edges of roof and sides.

4 Assemble levels 3 to 7. Glue together spire pieces. Wedge dowel piece into the top. Glue the skewer on to bobbin. Then glue bobbin on to dowel.

5 Glue spire on to top level. Use a thick brush to paint the base colour. Paint details, such as terracotta for the roof tiles, with a thin brush.

Houses and Gardens

living quarters for owner's immediate family

reception

watch tower

main courtyard

ALL BUILDINGS IN Chinese cities were designed to be in harmony with each other and with nature. The direction they faced, their layout and their proportions were all matters of great spiritual importance. Even the number of steps leading up to the entrance of the house was considered to be significant. House design in imperial China varied over time and between regions. In the hot and rainy south, courtyards tended to be covered for shade and shelter. In the drier climate of the north, courtyards were mostly open to the elements. Poor people in the countryside lived in simple, thatched huts. These were made from timber frames covered in mud plaster. They were often noisy, draughty and overcrowded. In contrast, the spacious homes of the wealthy were large, peaceful and well constructed. Many had beautiful gardens, filled with peonies, bamboo and wisteria. Some of these gardens also contained orchards, ponds and pavilions.

INSIDE A HAN HOUSE

A wealthy family go about their daily lives in a Han dynasty (206BC–AD220) home. The house is built around several courtyards, with a garden at the side and a gatehouse leading out into the streets. A watchtower gives a view of the world outside. The main family building at the rear is two storeys high, but some homes had three or more floors.

MAKE A HOUSE

You will need: thick cardboard, corrugated card, ruler, felt-tipped pen, scissors, glue and brush, 2.5cm x 5mm/1 x ¼in dowel (x 2), masking tape, paint (white, grey, pink), thick and thin paintbrushes, water pot.

Base — 28cm/11in × 24cm/9½in

Wall A — 25.5cm/10¼in, 2cm/¾in, 3cm/1¼in, 9cm/3¼in, 14.5cm/5¾in, 25.5cm/10¼in, 13.5cm/5¼in, 3cm/1¼in

Wall B (x 2) — 17cm/6⅓in, 13.5cm/5¼in

Stairs — 4cm/1½in, 2cm/¾in, 5.5cm/2¼in, 10.5cm/4¼in

Roof Piece A (x 4) — 18cm/7in, 7.5cm/3in

Gate — 7cm/2¾in, 5mm/¼in, 4cm/1½in

Wall C — 3cm/1¼in, 1.5cm/½in, 2cm/¾in, 12.5cm/4½in, 11.5cm/4¼in, 13.5cm, 3cm/1¼in

Wall D (x 2) — 11cm/4¼in, 8.5cm/3⅓in

Floor (x 2) — 6.5cm/2½in, 8.5cm/3½in, 15cm/6in, 7.5cm/3in

Roof Piece B (x 2) — 18cm/7in, 8cm/3½in

Wall E (x 2) — 8.5cm/3½in, 16cm/6¼in

Wall F (x2) — 9.5cm/3¾in, 18cm/7in, 7cm/2¾in, 9cm/3½in

Roof Bracket (x 6) — 7.5cm/3in, 4cm/1½in, 10.5cm/4¼in

Bend wall F here

1 Cut out card pieces. Glue walls A, E and F (bend F first) to base. Add floor and stairs. Glue dowel under floor. Glue corrugated card to stairs.

pond

garden

bridge

living quarters for other family members

round window

inner wall

horse and carriage

porch

gatehouse

outer wall

outer courtyard

ROOF CHARMS

Decorative dragons and animals guard the roof of the Lama Temple in Beijing. Many Chinese homes also featured exotic figures such as these. People believed that they would ward off evil spirits.

The design of this model is based on houses built in the south of China. The overhanging roofs cover the courtyard. This helps to keep out rain and to provide shelter from the sun.

2 To assemble second side, repeat method described in step 1. If necessary, hold pieces together with masking tape while the glue dries.

3 Glue B walls to the sides of the base, C wall to the back and D walls to the front. Hold with tape while glue dries. Glue gate between D walls.

4 Assemble A roofs (x 2) and B roof (x 1). Fix brackets underneath. Glue corrugated card (cut to same size as roof pieces) to top side of roofs.

5 Fix a small piece of card over the gate to make a porch. Paint house, as shown. Use a thin brush to create a tile effect on the removable roofs.

Home Comforts

A LARGE HOME in imperial China would include many living rooms for the owner and his wife, their children, the grandparents, and other members of the extended family. There were several kitchens, servants' quarters, and reception rooms where guests would dine. A wealthy scholar's home would even contain its own private library.

Clay stoves provided heat in the cold northern winters. Windows were made of either stiff paper or hemp sacking instead of glass. Walls were tiled, or else decorated with beautiful silk hangings. They could be extended with carved screens. In the early days of the empire, there would be low tables, stools, urns and vases. People slept on low, heated platforms called *kang* in northern China, and the floors of homes would be covered with various mats, rugs and cushions.

Furniture making developed rapidly during the Tang dynasty (AD618–906). Skilled craftsmen began producing beautiful furniture without using nails. Bamboo was widely used in the south. Instead of sitting at floor level, people began to use chairs and high tables. Elaborate furniture was made for the imperial palaces, using rosewood or woods inlaid with ivory or mother-of-pearl. Most people had furniture that was cheaper and simpler in design, but no less beautiful.

BRINGER OF LIGHT
This beautiful lamp is made of gilded bronze, and supported by the figure of a maidservant. It was found in the tomb of Liu Sheng, the Jade Prince. The lamp dates from about 100BC. At that time, homes were lit by oil-lamps or lanterns made of paper, silk or horn.

BEAUTY IN THE HOME
A delicate porcelain plate from the early 1700s shows a young woman standing by a table, leaning on the back of a chair. The neatly arranged books, scrolls and furniture show the importance the Chinese placed on order and harmony in the home. Chairs and tables were put against the walls. There was no clutter or mess, and possessions were always neatly put away.

FURNITURE AND FITTINGS
Richly embroidered hangings and carved tables decorate the office of this Chinese magistrate (c. 1600). Wealthy homes and the offices of important people often featured such luxurious decorations and furnishings.

GARDENS OF TRANQUILITY

Chinese gardens offered peace and beauty amidst the hustle and bustle of the city. Bamboo leaves rustled in the wind. Lotus flowers floated gracefully on ponds. Wisteria, with its tumbling blue flowers, wound around the summer houses. There were scented roses, peonies and chrysanthemums. Soft fruits, such as peaches and lychees, were also grown.

lychee

peach

DECORATIVE SCREEN

Standing behind the carved chair is a spectacular folding screen, made in the 1800s. Exotic paintings of landscapes, animals and birds cover its surface, while a glossy lacquer makes it smooth, hard and strong. Many wealthy homes had richly decorated wooden screens, while poorer ones had simpler, carved ones. Screens were used to keep rooms cool in summer and warm in winter.

KEEPING COOL

This wine vessel was made over 3,000 years ago. It was used to store wine for rituals and ceremonies. The vessel was made of bronze, which probably helped to chill the wine. Cooling the wine in this way would improve its taste.

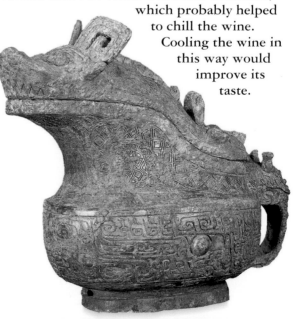

IMPERIAL AIR CONDITIONING

This beautifully decorated casket was formerly used in the Imperial Summer Palace, near Beijing. Its function was to hold blocks of ice to keep the air cool in the hot season. Its surface is inlaid with gold and other valuable materials. The perforated cover features a gilded bronze dragon design. The casket is supported by legs made in the shape of two kneeling figures.

Family Life

KONG FUZI (CONFUCIUS) taught that just as the emperor was head of the state, the oldest man was head of the household and should be obeyed by his family. In reality, his wife ran the home and often controlled the daily lives of the other women in the household.

During the Han dynasty (206BC–AD220) noblewomen were kept apart from the outside world. They could only gaze at the streets from the watchtowers of their homes. It was not until the Song dynasty (AD960–1279) that they gained more freedom. In poor households women worked all day, spending long, tiring hours farming, cooking, sweeping and washing.

For the children of poorer families, education meant learning to do the work their parents did. This involved carrying goods to market, or helping with the threshing or planting. The children of wealthier parents had private tutors at home. Boys hoping to become scholars or civil servants learned to read and write Chinese characters. They also studied maths and the works of Kong Fuzi.

LESSONS FOR THE BOYS
A group of Chinese boys take their school lessons. In imperial China, boys generally received a more academic education than girls. Girls were mainly taught music, handicrafts, painting and social skills. Some girls were taught academic subjects, but they were not allowed to sit the civil service examinations.

FOOT BINDING
This foot looks elegant in its beautiful slipper, but it's a different story when the slipper is removed. Just when life was improving for Chinese women, the cruel new custom of footbinding was introduced. Dancers had bound their feet for some years in the belief that it made them look dainty. In the Song dynasty the custom spread to wealthy and noble families. Little girls of five or so had their feet bound up so tightly that they became terribly deformed.

CHINESE MARRIAGE
A wedding ceremony takes place in the late 1800s. In imperial China, weddings were arranged by the parents of the bride and groom, rather than by the couples themselves. It was expected that the couple would respect their parents' wishes, even if they didn't like each other!

TAKING IT EASY

A noblewoman living during the Qing dynasty relaxes on a garden terrace with her children (c.1840). She is very fortunate as she has little else to do but enjoy the pleasant surroundings of her home. In rich families like hers, servants did most of the hard work, such as cooking, cleaning and washing. Wealthy Chinese families kept many servants, who usually lived in quarters inside their employer's home. Servants accounted for a large number of the workforce in imperial China. During the Ming dynasty (1368–1644), some 9,000 maidservants were employed at the imperial palace in Beijing alone!

RESPECT AND HONOUR

Children in the 1100s bow respectfully to their parents. Confucius taught that people should value and honour their families, including their ancestors. He believed that this helped to create a more orderly and virtuous society.

THE EMPEROR AND HIS MANY WIVES

Sui dynasty emperor Yangdi (AD581–618) rides out with his many womenfolk. Like many emperors, Yangdi was surrounded by women. An emperor married one woman, who would then become his empress, but he would still enjoy the company of concubines (secondary wives).

Farming and Crops

EIGHT THOUSAND YEARS AGO most Chinese people were already living by farming. The best soil lay beside the great rivers in central and eastern China, where floods left behind rich, fertile mud. As today, wheat and millet were grown in the north. This region was mostly farmed by peasants with small plots of land. Rice was cultivated in the warm, wet south, where wealthy city-dwellers owned large estates. Pears and oranges were grown in orchards.

Tea, later to become one of China's most famous exports, was first cultivated about 1,700 years ago. Hemp was also grown for its fibres. During the 500s BC, cotton was introduced. Farmers raised pigs, ducks, chickens and geese, while oxen and water buffalo were used as labouring animals on the farm.

Most peasants used basic tools, such as stone hoes and wooden rakes. Ploughs with iron blades were used from about 600BC. Other inventions to help farmers were developed in the next few hundred years, including the wheelbarrow, a pedal hammer for husking grain and a rotary winnowing fan.

PIGS ARE FARM FAVOURITES
This pottery model of pigs in their sty dates back about 2,000 years. Pigs were popular farm animals, as they are easy to feed and most parts of a pig can be eaten. They were kept in the city as well as in rural country areas.

FEEDING THE MANY
Rice has been grown in the wetter regions of China since ancient times. Wheat and millet are grown in the drier regions. Sprouts of the Indian mung bean add important vitamins to many dishes.

mung beans

millet

rice

wheat

CHINESE TEAS
Delicate leaves of tea are picked from the bushes and gathered in large baskets on this estate in the 1800s. The Chinese cultivated tea in ancient times, but it became much more popular during the Tang dynasty (AD618–906). The leaves were picked, laid out in the sun, rolled by hand and then dried over charcoal fires.

WORKING THE LAND

A farmer uses a pair of strong oxen to help him plough his land. This wall painting found in Jiayuguan dates back to about 100BC. Oxen saved farmers a lot of time and effort. The Chinese first used oxen in farming in about 1122BC.

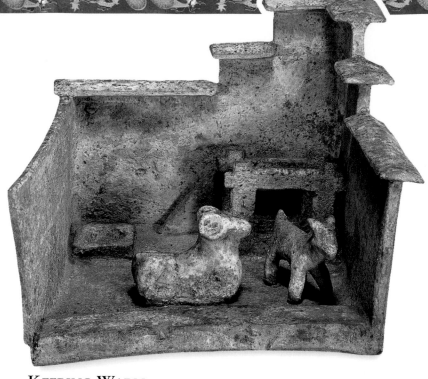

KEEPING WARM

This model of a Chinese farmer's lambing shed dates from about 100BC, during the Han dynasty. Sheepskins were worn for warmth, but wool never became an important textile for clothes or blankets in China.

HARVESTING RICE – CHINA'S MAIN FOOD

Chinese peasants pull up rice plants for threshing and winnowing in the 1600s. Farming methods were passed on by word of mouth and in handbooks from the earliest times. They advised farmers on everything from fertilizing the soil to controlling pests.

A TIMELESS SCENE

Peasants bend over to plant out rows of rice seedlings in the flooded paddy fields of Yunnan province, in southwest China. This modern photograph is a typical scene of agricultural life in China's warm and wet southwest region. Little has changed in hundreds of years of farming.

Fine Food

CHINESE COOKS TODAY are among the best in the world, with skills gained over thousands of years. Rice was the basis of most meals in ancient China, especially in the south where it was grown. Northerners used wheat flour to make noodles and buns. Food varied greatly between the regions. The north was famous for pancakes, dumplings, lamb and duck dishes. In the west, Sichuan was renowned for its hot chilli peppers. Mushrooms and bamboo shoots were popular along the lower Chang Jiang (Yangzi River).

For many people, meat was a rare treat. It included chicken, pork and many kinds of fish, and was often spiced with garlic and ginger. Dishes featured meat that people from other parts of the world might find strange, such as turtle, dog, monkey and bear. Food was stewed, steamed or fried. The use of chopsticks and bowls dates back to the Shang dynasty (*c.*1600–1122BC).

THE KITCHEN GOD
In every kitchen hung a paper picture of the kitchen god and his wife. Each year, on the 24th day of the 12th month, sweets (candies) were put out as offerings. Then the picture was taken down and burned. A new one was put in its place on New Year's Day.

A TANG BANQUET
These elegant ladies of the Tang court are sitting down to a feast. They are accompanied by music and singing, but there are no men present – women and men usually ate separately. This painting dates from the AD900s, when raised tables came into fashion in China. Guests at banquets would wear their finest clothes. The most honoured guest would sit to the east of the host, who sat facing the south. The greatest honour of all was to be invited to dine with the emperor.

MAKE RED BEAN SOUP
You will need: scales, 225g/½lb/ 1¼ cups aduki beans, 15ml/3 tsp ground nuts, 20ml/4 tsp short grain rice, jug (cup), water, bowl, tangerine, pan and lid, wooden spoon, 150g/5oz/¾ cup sugar, liquidizer, sieve (strainer), bowls.

1 Use the scales to weigh out the aduki beans. Add the ground nuts and the short grain rice. Measure out 1 litre/1¾ pints/ 4 cups of water in the jug.

2 Wash and drain the beans, nuts and rice. Put them in a bowl. Add the cold water. Leave overnight to soak. Do not drain off the water.

3 Wash and dry the tangerine. Then carefully take off the peel in a continuous strip. Leave the peel overnight, until it is hard and dry.

THAT SPECIAL TASTE

Garlic has been used to flavour Chinese dishes and sauces for thousands of years. It may be chopped, crushed, pickled or served whole. Root ginger is another crucial Chinese taste. Fresh chilli peppers are used to make fiery dishes, while sesame provides flavouring in the form of paste, oil and seeds.

sesame   *root ginger*

SHANG BRONZEWARE FIT FOR A FEAST

This three-legged bronze cooking pot dates from the Shang dynasty (*c.*1600BC–1122BC). Its green appearance is caused by the reaction of the metal to air over the 3,500 years since it was made. During Shang rule, metalworkers made many vessels out of bronze, including cooking pots and wine jars. They were used in all sorts of ceremonies, and at feasts people held in honour of their dead ancestors.

BUTCHERS AT WORK

The stone carving *(shown right)* shows farmers butchering cattle in about AD50. In early China, cooks would cut up meat with square-shaped cleavers. It was then flavoured with wines and spices, and simmered in big pots over open fires until tender.

Most peasant farmers lived on a simple diet. Red bean soup with rice was a typical daily meal. Herbs and spices were often added to make the food taste more interesting.

4 Put the soaked beans, nuts and rice (plus the liquid) into a large pan. Add the dried tangerine peel and 500ml/17fl oz/ generous 2 cups of cold water.

5 Bring the mixture to the boil. Reduce the heat, cover the pan and simmer for 2 hours. Stir occasionally. If the liquid boils off, add more water.

6 Weigh out the sugar. When the beans are just covered by water, add the sugar. Simmer until the sugar has completely dissolved.

7 Remove and discard the peel. Leave the soup to cool, uncovered. Liquidize the mixture. Strain any lumps with a sieve. Pour into bowls.

Markets and Trade

THE EARLIEST CHINESE TRADERS used to barter (exchange) goods, but by 1600BC people were finding it easier to use tokens such as shells for buying and selling. The first metal coins date from about 750BC and were shaped like knives and spades. It was Qin Shi Huangdi, the first emperor, who introduced round coins. These had holes in the middle so that they could be threaded on to a cord for safe-keeping. The world's first paper money appeared in China in about AD900.

There were busy markets in every Chinese town, selling fruit, vegetables, rice, flour, eggs and poultry as well as cloth, medicine, pots and pans. In the Tang dynasty capital Chang'an (Xian), trading was limited to two large areas – the West Market and the East Market. This was so that government officials could control prices and trading standards.

CHINESE TRADING
Goods from China changed hands many times on the Silk Road to Europe. Trade moved in both directions. Porcelain, tea and silk were carried westwards. Silver, gold and precious stones were transported back into China from central and southern Asia.

raw silk

Chinese tea

CASH CROPS
Tea is trampled into chests in this European view of tea production in China. The work looks hard and the conditions cramped. For years China had traded with India and Arabia. In the 1500s it began a continuous trading relationship with Europe. By the early 1800s, China supplied 90 per cent of all the world's tea.

MAKE A PELLET DRUM

You will need: large roll of masking tape, pencil, thin cream card, thick cardboard, scissors, glue and brush, 2.5 x 30cm/1 x 12in strip of thin grey card, 2 x 20cm/ 8in threads, ruler, needle, bamboo stick, paint (red, green and black), water pot, brush, 2 coloured beads.

1 Use the outside of the roll of tape to draw two circles on thin cream card. Use the inside to draw two smaller circles on thick card. Cut out, as shown.

2 Glue the strip of grey card around one of the smaller circles. Make two holes each side of the strip. Pass the threads through the holes and knot.

3 Use the scissors to make a hole in the side of the strip for the bamboo stick. Push the stick through, as shown. Tape the stick to the hole.

THE SILK ROAD

The trading route known as the Silk Road developed during the Han dynasty. The road ran for 11,000km/6,800 miles from Chang'an (modern Xian), through Yumen and Kasghar, to Persia and the shores of the Mediterranean Sea. Merchants carried tea, silk and other goods from one trading post to the next.

FROM DISTANT LANDS

A foreign trader rides on his camel during the Tang dynasty. At this time, China's international trade began to grow rapidly. Most trade was still handled by foreign merchants, among them Armenians, Jews and Persians. They traded their wares along the Silk Road, bringing goods to the court at the Tang dynasty capital, Chang'an.

BUYERS AND SELLERS

This picture shows a typical Chinese market in about 1100. It appears on a Song dynasty scroll and is thought to show the market in the capital, Kaifeng, at the time of the New Year festival.

Twist the drum handle to make the little balls rattle. In the hubbub of a street market, a merchant could shake a pellet drum to gain the attention of passers by. He would literally drum up trade!

4 Tape the stick handle down securely at the top of the drum. Take the second small circle and glue it firmly into place. This seals the drum.

5 Draw matching designs of your choice on the two thin cream card circles. Cut out a decorative edge. Paint in the designs and leave them to dry.

6 Paint the bamboo stick handle red and leave to dry. When the stick is dry, glue the decorated circles into position on top of the two smaller circles.

7 Thread on the two beads. Make sure the thread is long enough to allow the beads to hit the centre of the drum. Tie as shown. Cut off any excess.

Medicine and Science

FROM THE EMPIRE'S earliest days, Chinese scholars published studies on medicine, astronomy and mathematics. The Chinese system of medicine had a similar aim to that of Daoist teachings, in that it attempted to make the body work harmoniously. The effects of all kinds of herbs, plants and animal parts were studied and then used to produce medicines. Acupuncture, which involves piercing the body with fine needles, was practised from about 2700BC. It was believed to release blocked channels of energy and so relieve pain.

The Chinese were also excellent mathematicians, and from 300BC they used a decimal system of counting based on tens. They may have invented the abacus, an early form of calculator, as well. In about 3000BC, Chinese astronomers produced a detailed chart of the heavens carved in stone. Later, they were the first to make observations of sunspots and exploding stars.

NEW ILLS, OLD REMEDIES
A pharmacist weighs out a traditional medicine. Hundreds of medicines used in China today go back to ancient times. Many are herbal remedies later proved to work by scientists. Doctors are still researching their uses. Other traditional medicines are of less certain value, but are still popular purchases at street stalls.

PRICKING POINTS
Acupuncturists used charts (*shown above*) to show exactly where to position their needles. The vital *qi* (energy) was thought to flow through the body along 12 lines called meridians. The health of the patient was judged by taking their pulse. Chinese acupuncture is practised all over the world today.

MAKE AN ABACUS

You will need: thick and thin card, ruler, pencil, scissors, wood glue and brush, masking tape, self-hardening clay, cutting board, modelling tool, 30cm x 5mm/12 x ¼in pieces of dowel (x 11), paintbrush, water pot, brown paint.

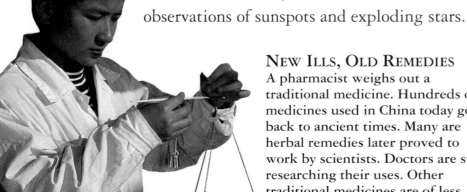

Side A (x 2) — 32cm/12¾in — 3cm/1¼in
Edge A (x 2) — 32cm/12¾in / 30cm/12in — 5mm/¼in
Side B (x 2) — 16cm/6¼in — 3cm/1¼in
Edge B (x 2) — 16cm/6¼in / 15cm/6in — 5mm/¼in
Divider — 30cm/12in — Divider edge
Base — 32cm/12¾in — 16cm/6¼in — 3cm/1¼in — 5mm/¼in

Using the measurements above, cut out pieces from thick brown card and thin grey card. (Pieces not shown to scale).

1 Glue sides A and B to the base. Hold the edges with masking tape until dry. Then glue edges A and B to the tops of the sides, as shown.

2 Roll the clay into a 2cm/⅜in-diameter sausage shape. Cut it into 77 small, flat beads. Make a hole through the middle of each bead with a dowel.

A STREET DOCTOR PEDDLES HIS WARES
This European view of Chinese medicine dates from 1843.
It shows snakes and all sorts of unusual potions being sold on
the streets. The doctor is telling the crowd of miraculous cures.

NATURAL HEALTH
Roots, seeds, leaves and flowers
have been used in Chinese medicine
for over 2,000 years. Today, nine out
of ten Chinese medicines are herbal
remedies. The Chinese yam is used
to treat exhaustion. Ginseng root is
used to help treat dizzy spells,
while mulberry wood is said to
lower blood pressure.

Chinese yam

*ginseng
root*

BURNING CURES
A country doctor
treats a patient with
traditional techniques
during the Song
dynasty. Chinese
doctors relieved pain
by heating parts of the
body with the burning
leaves of a plant called
moxa (mugwort).
The process is
called moxibustion.

*The abacus is an ancient
counting frame that acts as
a simple but very effective
calculator. Using an abacus,
Chinese mathematicians
and merchants could carry
out very difficult
calculations quickly
and easily.*

3 Make 11 evenly spaced holes
in the divider. Edge one side
with thin card. Thread a dowel
through each hole. Paint all of
the abacus parts. Leave to dry.

4 Thread seven beads on to
each rod – two on the upper
side of the divider, five on the
lower. Carefully fit the beads
and rods into the main frame.

5 Each upper bead equals five
lower beads in the same
column. Each lower bead is
worth 10 of the lower beads
in the column to its right.

6 Here is a sum. To calculate
5+3, first move down one
upper bead (worth 5). Then
move three lower beads in the
same column up (each worth 1).

Feats of Engineering

THE ENGINEERING WONDER of ancient China was the Great Wall. It was known as *Wan Li Chang Cheng*, or the Wall of Ten Thousand *Li* (a unit of length). The Great Wall's main length was an incredible 4,000km/2,485 miles. Work began on the wall in the 400s BC and lasted until the AD1500s. Its purpose was to protect China's borders from the fierce tribes who lived to the north. Despite this intention, Mongol invaders managed to breach its defences time after time. However, the Great Wall did serve as a useful communications route. It also extended the Chinese empire's control over a very long distance.

The Grand Canal is another engineering project that amazes us today. It was started in the 400s BC, but was mostly built during the Sui dynasty (AD581–618). Its aim was to link the north of China with the rice-growing regions in the south via the Chang Jiang (Yangzi River). It is still in use and runs northwards from Hangzhou to Beijing, a distance of 1,794km/1,115 miles. Other great engineering feats were made by Chinese mining engineers, who were already digging deep mine shafts with drainage and ventilation systems in about 160BC.

LIFE IN THE SALT MINES
Workers busily excavate and purify salt from an underground mine. Inside a tower (*shown bottom left*) you can see workers using a pulley to raise baskets of mined salt. The picture comes from a relief (raised carving) found inside a Han dynasty tomb in the province of Sichuan.

MINING ENGINEERING
A Qing dynasty official tours an open-cast coalmine in the 1800s. China has rich natural resources and may have been the first country in the world to mine coal to burn as a fuel. Coal was probably discovered in about 200BC in what is now Jiangxi province. Other mines extracted metals and valuable minerals needed for the great empire. In the Han dynasty engineers invented methods of drilling boreholes to extract brine (salty water) from the ground. They also used derricks (rigid frameworks) to support iron drills – over 1,800 years before engineers in other parts of the world.

HARD LABOUR

Peasants use their spades to dig roads instead of fields. Imperial China produced its great building and engineering works without the machines we rely on today. For big projects, workforces could number hundreds of thousands. Dangerous working conditions and a harsh climate killed many labourers.

BUILDING THE WALL

The Great Wall snakes over mountain ridges at Badaling, to the northwest of Beijing. The Great Wall and Grand Canal were built by millions of workers. All men aged between 23 and 56 were called up to work on them for one month each year. Only noblemen and civil servants were exempt.

A GRAND OPENING

This painting from the 1700s imagines the Sui emperor Yangdi opening the first stage of the Grand Canal. Most of the work on this massive engineering project was carried out from AD605–609. A road was also built along the route. The transport network built up during the Sui dynasty (AD561–618) enabled food and other supplies to be moved easily from one part of the empire to another.

THE CITY OF SIX THOUSAND BRIDGES

The reports about China supposedly made by Marco Polo in the 1200s described 6,000 bridges in the city of Suzhou. The Baodai Bridge *(shown above)* is one of them. It has 53 arches and was built between AD618 and AD906 to run across the Grand Canal.

Famous Inventions

WHEN YOU WALK DOWN a shopping street in any modern city, it is very difficult to avoid seeing some object that was invented in China long ago. Printed words on paper, silk scarves, umbrellas or locks and keys are all Chinese innovations. Over the centuries, Chinese ingenuity and technical skill have changed the world in which we live.

A seismoscope is a very useful instrument in an earthquake-prone country such as China. It was invented in AD132 by a Chinese scientist called Zhang Heng. It could record the direction of even a distant earth tremor. Another key invention was the magnetic compass. In about AD1–100 the Chinese discovered that lodestone (a type of iron ore) could be made to point north. They realized that they could magnetize needles to do the same. By about AD1000, they worked out the difference between true north and magnetic north and began using compasses to keep ships on course.

Gunpowder is a Chinese invention from about AD850. At first it was used to blast rocks apart and to make fireworks. Later, it also began to be used in warfare.

SHADE AND SHELTER
A Qing dynasty woman uses an umbrella as a sunshade to protect her skin. The Chinese invented umbrellas about 1,600 years ago and they soon spread throughout the rest of Asia. Umbrellas became fashionable with both women and men and were regarded as a symbol of high rank.

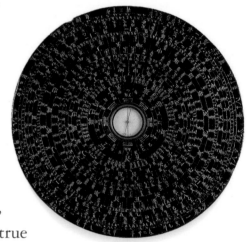

THE SAILOR'S FRIEND
The magnetic compass was invented in China in about AD1–100. At first it was used as a planning aid to ensure new houses faced in a direction that was in harmony with nature. Later it was used to plot courses on long sea voyages.

MAKE A WHEELBARROW
You will need: thick cardboard, ruler, pencil, scissors, pair of compasses, 5mm/¼in-diameter balsa wood cut into strips 7cm/2¾in, 8cm/3¼in and 26cm/10¼in (x 2) long, glue and brush, paintbrush, paint (black and brown), water pot, 3.5cm x 5mm/ 1¼ x ¼in dowel, 2cm/¾in-diameter rubber washers (x 4).

Base — 8cm/3¼in — 2.5cm/1in — 11cm/4½in — 15cm/6in — 3cm/1¼in — 2cm/¾in

Wheel — 10cm/4in — 1.5cm/½in

Using the measurements above, draw the pieces on to thick card. Draw the wheel with a pair of compasses. Cut out with scissors.

1 Glue the 7cm/2¾in balsa strip to the short edge of base and the 8cm/3¼in strip to the top edge. Glue the 26cm/10¼in strips to the sides of the base.

SU SONG'S MASTERPIECE

This fantastic machine is a clock tower that can tell the time, chime the hours and follow the movement of the planets around the Sun. It was designed by an official called Su Song, in the city of Kaifeng in AD1092. The machine uses a mechanism called an escapement, which controls and regulates the timing of the clock. The escapement mechanism was invented in the AD700s by a Chinese inventor called Yi Xing.

EARTHQUAKE WARNING

The decorative object shown above is the scientist Zhang Heng's seismoscope. When there was an earthquake, a ball was released from one of the dragons and fell into a frog's mouth. This showed the direction of the vibrations. According to records, in AD138 the instrument detected a earth tremor some 500km/310 miles away.

ONE-WHEELED TRANSPORT

In about AD100, the Chinese invented the wheelbarrow. They then designed a model with a large central wheel that could bear great weights. This became a form of transport, pushed along by muscle power.

The single wheelbarrow was used by farmers and gardeners. Traders wheeled their goods to market, then used the barrow as a stall. They would sell a variety of goods, such as seeds, grain, plants and dried herbs.

2 Turn the base over. Cut two 2 x 1cm/¾ x ½in pieces of thick card. Make a small hole in the middle of each, for the wheel axle. Glue pieces to base.

3 Use a pair of compasses to draw one circle around the centre of the wheel and one near the rim. Mark on spokes. Paint spaces between spokes black.

4 Paint the barrow and leave to dry. Cut two 7cm/2¾in balsa strips with tapered ends to make legs. Paint brown. When dry, glue to bottom of barrow.

5 Feed dowel axle between axle supports, via two washers, a wheel, and two more washers. Dab glue on ends of axle, so wheel spins without falling off.

Stone Relics

CHINESE CIVILIZATION BEGAN over 5,000 years ago in the Neolithic period (New Stone Age). Stone was one of the first materials to be worked. It was used to make practical objects, such as hand mills for grinding grain or tools for the farm, as well as for ornaments.

The Chinese valued one type of stone above all others – jade. Many figures and statues were made of the stone. People thought it had magical properties and could preserve the dead. The Han dynasty prince Liu Sheng and his wife, Dou Wan, were buried in suits made of over 2,000 thin jade plates sewn together with gold wire.

On a very different scale, the spread of Buddhism led to the popularity of gigantic stone sculptures. The Great Buddha above the town of Leshan, Sichuan, was carved into the rock in the AD700s. It is 70m/230ft high and took 90 years to carve from the rockface. Inside, a system of drains helps to prevent the stone from weathering.

BUFFALO IN JADE
Water buffalo were highly prized animals in imperial China. This beautiful carving measures about 43cm/17in in length. It was carved from a single large piece of jade during the 1300s. The precious stone was mined in the northwest of the country, in the region that is now known as Xinjiang.

STONY ELEPHANT
An uncomfortable-looking elephant (*shown above*) is one of many statues of animals that line the 7km/4½ miles of the Spirit Way. This is a ceremonial avenue that leads to the Ming tombs at Shisanling, to the north of Beijing. The elephant statue was carved during the 1400s.

FOLLY IN MARBLE
A Mississippi paddle steamer was the model for this fake boat. It will never sail, as it is made of marble. It was built in the last days of the empire for Empress Dowager Cixi. She used funds meant for the navy to build it at her Summer Palace in Yiheyuan.

THE AFTERLIFE

This stone statue is one of many that guard the tombs at Shisanling, north of Beijing. Yong Li and 12 other Ming emperors were buried here from the 1400s onwards. The statues were made in the form of both humans and animals. They were probably placed there to protect each emperor in his next life.

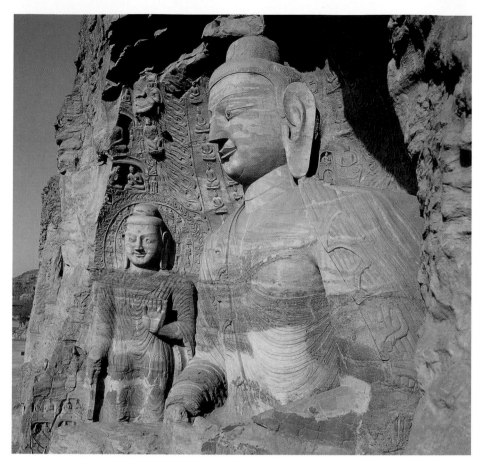

CARVED FROM ROCK

A great Buddha dominates the spectacular stone carvings of the Yungang cave temples. It is located in what is now Shanxi province, northern China. The huge figure is some 15m/49ft in height. The elaborate stone carvings at the caves were completed at some point between AD460 and the early AD500s. In total, they take up 1km/½ mile of the rockface.

JADE AXEHEAD

Simple decorative notches are carved on to this Shang dynasty jade axehead. Jade is a tough and difficult stone to cut. Early craftsmen did not have sharp enough tools to cut more detailed or elaborate patterns.

JADE DISCS

Bi are large discs made of jade. The one shown here measures about 27cm/10½in in diameter. *Bi* were usually hung from cords of silk and were meant to represent heaven. These patterned discs were worn by priests at ceremonies from about 2500BC until Han times.

Workers of Metal

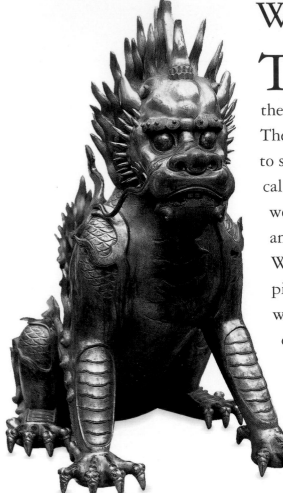

BEWARE OF THE LION
This gilded *fo* (Buddhist) lion guards the halls and chambers of Beijing's imperial palace, the Forbidden City. It is one of a fearsome collection of bronze guardian figures, including statues of dragons and turtles.

THE CHINESE MASTERED THE secrets of making alloys (mixtures of two or more metals) during the Shang dynasty (*c*.1600BC–1122BC). They made bronze by melting copper and tin to separate each metal from its ore, a process called smelting. Nine parts of copper were then mixed with one part of tin and heated in a charcoal furnace. When the metals melted they were piped off into clay moulds. Bronze was used to make objects such as ceremonial pots, statues, bells, mirrors, tools and weapons.

By about 600BC the Chinese were smelting iron ore. They then became the first people to make cast iron by adding carbon to the molten metal.

SILVER SCISSORS
This pair of scissors is made of silver. They are proof of the foreign influences that entered China in the AD700s, during the boom years of the Tang dynasty. The metal is beaten, rather than cast in the Chinese way. It is decorated in the Persian style of the Silk Road, with engraving and punching.

Cast iron is a tougher metal than bronze and it was soon being used to make weapons, tools and plough blades. By AD1000 the Chinese were mining and working a vast amount of iron. Coke (a type of coal) had replaced the charcoal used in furnaces, which were fired up by water-driven bellows. Chinese metal workers also produced delicate gold and silver ornaments set with precious stones.

MAKE A NECKLACE

You will need: tape measure, thick wire, thin wire, masking tape, scissors, foil, measuring spoon, glue and brush, fuse wire.

1 Measure around your neck using a tape measure. Ask an adult to cut a piece of thick wire to 1½ times this length. Shape it into a rough circle.

2 Cut two 4cm/1½in pieces of thin wire. Coil loosely around sides of thick wire. Tape ends to thick wire. Slide thick wire through coils to adjust fit.

3 Cut out an oval-shaped piece of foil. Shape it into a pendant half, using a measuring spoon or teaspoon. Make nine more halves.

MINERAL WEALTH

The Chinese probably learnt to smelt ore in furnaces from their experience with high-temperature pottery kilns. The land was rich in copper, tin and iron, and the Chinese were very skilled miners. Large amounts of precious metals, such as gold and silver, had to be imported.

gold nugget   *silver ore*

PEACE BE WITH YOU

The Hall of Supreme Harmony in Beijing's Forbidden City is guarded by this bronze statue of a turtle. Despite its rather fearsome appearance, the turtle was actually a symbol of peace.

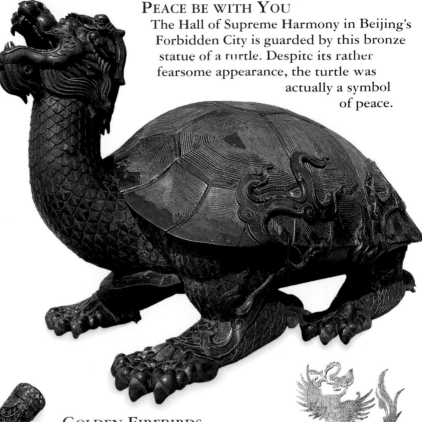

DECORATIVE PROTECTION

These nail protectors are made of gold, with inlaid feathers. They were worn by the Empress Dowager Cixi in the 1800s to stop her 15cm/6in-long little fingernails breaking.

GOLDEN FIREBIRDS

Chinese craftsmen fashioned these beautiful phoenix birds from thin sheets of delicate gold. The mythical Arabian phoenix was said to set fire to its nest and die, only to rise again from the ashes. During the Tang dynasty the phoenix became a symbol of the Chinese empress Wu Zetian, who came to power in AD660. It later came to be a more general symbol for all empresses.

4 Glue the two pendant halves together, leaving one end open. Drop some rolled-up balls of foil into the opening. Seal the opening with glue.

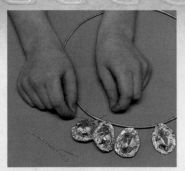

5 Make four more pendants in the same way. Thread each pendant on to the neckband with pieces of thin fuse wire. Leave a gap between each one.

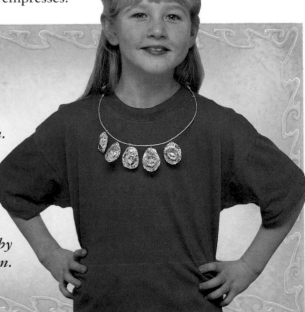

People of all classes wore decorative jewellery in imperial China. The design of this necklace is based on the metal bell bracelets worn by Chinese children.

Porcelain and Lacquer

ALTHOUGH POTTERY FIRST developed in Japan and parts of western Asia, Chinese potters were hard at work over 6,000 years ago. In 3200BC, clay was being fired (baked) in kilns at about 900°C/1,600°F. By 1400BC, potters were making beautiful, white stoneware, baked at much higher temperatures. Shiny glazes were developed to coat the fired clay. Later, the Chinese invented porcelain, the finest, most delicate pottery of all. It was to become one of China's most important exports to other parts of Asia and Europe. In the English language, the word china is used for all fine-quality pottery.

The Chinese were the first to use lacquer. This plastic-like material is a natural substance from the sap of a tree that grows in China. The sap makes a smooth, hard varnish. From about 1300BC onwards, lacquer was used for coating wooden surfaces, such as house timbers, bowls or furniture. It could also be applied to leather and metal. Natural lacquer is grey, but in China pigment was added to make it black or bright red. It was applied in many layers until thick enough to be carved or inlaid with mother-of-pearl.

ENAMEL WARE
Ming dynasty craft workers made this ornate flask. It is covered with a glassy material called enamel, set inside thin metal wire. This technique, called cloisonné (partitioned), was introduced from Persia.

CHINA'S HISTORY TOLD ON THE BIG SCREEN
This beautifully detailed, glossy lacquer screen shows a group of Portuguese merchants on a visit to China. It was made in the 1600s. Chinese crafts first became popular in Europe at this time, as European traders began doing business in southern China's ports.

FLORAL BOTTLE
This attractive Ming dynasty bottle is decorated with a coating of bright red lacquer. The lacquer is coloured with a mineral called cinnabar. It would have taken many long hours to apply and dry the many layers of lacquer. The bottle is carved with a design of peonies, which were a very popular flower in China.

FISH ON A PLATE

Pictures of fish decorate the border of this precious porcelain plate. It was made during the reign of the Qing emperor Yongzheng (1722–1736), a period famous for its elegant designs. It is coloured with enamel. Porcelain is made from a fine white clay called kaolin (china clay) and a mineral called feldspar. They are fired (baked) to a very high temperature.

A JUG OF WINE

An unknown Chinese potter made this beautiful wine jug (pitcher) about 1,000 years ago. It has been fired to such a high temperature that it has become glassy stoneware. It is coated with a grey-green glaze called celadon.

LIFE-LIKE FIGURES

A Ming dynasty entertainer smiles at his audience. All sorts of pottery figures have been found in Ming dynasty tombs. Potters made lively figures of merchants, musicians, court ladies and animals. Some are comic, while others are beautiful.

DEEP BLUE, PURE WHITE

These blue-and-white vases are typical of the late Ming dynasty (1368–1644). In the 1600s large numbers were exported to Europe. Many were produced at the imperial potteries at Jingdezhen, in northern Jiangxi province. These workshops were set up in 1369, as the region had plentiful supplies of the very best clay. Some of the finest pottery ever made was produced there in the 1400s and 1500s.

The Secret of Silk

FOR YEARS, THE CHINESE tried to stop outsiders finding out how they made their most popular export – *si*, or silk. The shimmering colours and smooth textures of Chinese silk made it the wonder of the ancient world. Other countries such as India discovered the secret of silk-making, but China remained the producer of the world's best silk.

Silk production probably dates back to late Stone Age times (8000–2500BC) in China. Legend says that the process was invented by the empress Lei Zu in about 2640BC. Silkworms (the caterpillars of a type of moth) are kept on trays and fed on the leaves of white mulberry trees. The silkworms spin a cocoon (casing) of fine but very strong filaments. The cocoons are plunged into boiling water to separate the filaments, which are then carefully wound on to reels.

A filament of silk can be up to 1,200m/4,000ft long. Several filaments are spun together to make up thread, which is then woven into cloth on a loom. The Chinese used silk to make all kinds of beautiful products. They learned to weave flimsy gauzes and rich brocades, and they then wove elaborate coloured patterns into the cloth in a style known as *ke si*, or 'cut silk'.

PREPARING THE THREAD
A young woman winds silk thread on to bobbins in the late 1700s. Up to 30 filaments of silk could be twisted together to make silk thread for weaving. The Chinese made ingenious equipment for spinning silk into thread. They also built looms for weaving thread into large rolls of fabric. By the 1600s, the city of Nanjing alone had an estimated 50,000 looms.

LOAD THOSE BALES!
Workers at a Chinese silk factory of the 1840s carry large bales of woven silk down to the jetty. From there the woven cloth would be shipped to the city. It might be used to make a costume for a lady of the court, or else exported abroad. The Chinese silk industry reached its peak of prosperity in the mid-1800s.

THE DRAGON ON THE EMPEROR'S BACK
A scaly red dragon writhes across a sea of yellow silk. The dragon was embroidered on to a robe for an emperor of the Qing dynasty. The exquisite clothes made for the Chinese imperial court at this time are considered to be great works of art.

WINDING SILK
Silk is being prepared at this workshop of the 1600s. The workers are taking filaments (threads) from the cocoons and winding them on to a reel. Traditionally, the chief areas of silk production in imperial China were in the east coast provinces of Zhejiang and Jiangsu. Silk was also produced in large quantities in Sichuan, in the west.

MAGIC MULBERRIES
These Han dynasty workers are collecting mulberry leaves in big baskets, over 2,000 years ago. These would have been used to feed the silkworms. Silkworms are actually the larva (caterpillars) of a kind of moth. Like most caterpillars, silkworms are fussy feeders and will only eat certain kinds of plant before they spin cocoons.

MAKING SILK
Raising silkworms is called sericulture. It can be a complicated business. The caterpillars have to be kept at a controlled temperature for a month before they begin spinning their silk cocoons.

adult silkmoth and cocoons

silkmoth larva

Dress and Ornament

CHINESE PEASANTS dressed in simple clothes made from basic materials. They mostly wore cotton tunics over loose trousers, with sandals made of rushes or straw. In the south, broad-brimmed, cone-shaped hats helped to protect the wearer from the hot sun and heavy rain. In the north, fur hats, sheepskins and quilted jackets were worn to keep out the cold.

Rich people often dressed in elaborate, expensive clothes. Government officials wore special robes that reflected their rank and status. Beautiful silk robes patterned with dragons (*lung pao*) were worn by court ladies, officials, and the emperor himself.

CLOTHES FIT FOR AN EMPEROR
This magnificent imperial robe was made from interwoven, heavy silks in the 1800s. The narrow sleeves, with their horse hoof cuffs, are typical of the Qing dynasty.

MONKEY PENDANT
Wealthy people often wore very expensive, well-crafted jewellery. This beautiful piece from the AD700s is a pendant necklace. It could have been worn by both men and women. The pendant is made from white jade set in a beaded frame of gilded bronze.

Court dress varied greatly over the ages. Foreign invasions brought new fashions and dress codes. Under the Manchus, who ruled as the Qing dynasty from AD1644, men had to wear a long pigtail. Rich people grew their little fingernails so long that special nail guards were worn to prevent them from breaking off.

FASTEN YOUR BELT
Belt hooks and buckles became an essential part of noblemen's clothing from about the 300s BC. They were highly decorated, and made of bronze.

MAKE A FAN

You will need: masking tape, red tissue paper, thick cardboard base, ruler, pencil, pair of compasses, paint (pink, light blue, cream, light green), thin paintbrush, water pot, scissors, 16 x 1cm/6¼ x ½in balsa strips (x 15), wooden skewer, glue and brush, thin card.

1 Tape tissue paper on the base. Make a compass hole 1cm/½in from the edge. From this, draw semicircles with radiuses of 16cm/6¼in and 7cm/2¾in.

2 Place one end of the ruler at the compass hole. Mark the point with a pencil. Draw evenly spaced lines 1cm/½in apart between the semicircles.

3 Draw your design on to the tissue paper. Paint in the details. Allow to dry. Remove paper from base. Cut out fan along edges of the semicircles.

OFFICIAL DRESS

A well-dressed civil servant cools down in the summer heat. Chinese government officials wore elegant clothes that showed their social rank. This picture was painted by a European artist in about 1800. The official is wearing his summer outfit, which consists of a long narrow-sleeved tunic, slippers and a brimmed hat. It is a hot day, so he also carries a fan to provide a cool breeze.

LADIES OF THE COURT

These Tang ladies are dressed in the high fashion of the AD700s. Silk was the material worn by the nobles of the day, and court costume included long robes and skirts, various tunics and sashes. The clothes were often beautifully decorated, with bright patterns and elaborate designs.

ADDED STYLE

Over the ages, all kinds of accessories became part of Chinese costume. These included elaborate hats and headdresses for men and women, sunshades, fans, belts and buckles. Tiny leather shoes lined with silk were worn by noble women.

ladies' shoes

fans

earring

back of fan

The earliest Chinese fans were made of feathers or of silk stretched over a flat frame. In about AD1000 folding fans were introduced into China, probably from Japan.

4 Using scissors, cut each balsa strip 1cm/½in narrower (5mm/¼in each side) for half of its length. Make a compass hole at the base of each strip.

5 Stack strips. Pass a skewer through the holes. It must be long enough to fit through and overlap either side. Make sure the strips can move freely.

6 Fold the paper backwards and forwards to form a concertina. Glue each alternate fold of the paper to the narrow ends of the strips, as shown.

7 Paint the top strip of the fan pink. Allow to dry. Cut out small card circles. Glue them over the ends of the skewer to secure the strips.

Chinese Art

IN IMPERIAL CHINA, painting was believed to be the finest of all the arts. It was considered to be a mark of civilization and a suitable pastime for scholars and even emperors. Painting was based upon the same ideas of harmony and simplicity that were important in the Daoist and Buddhist faiths. Paintings appeared on scrolls of silk and paper, walls, screens and fans. Popular subjects for pictures varied over the ages. They included the misty mountains and rivers of southern China, as well as landscapes set off by lone human figures. Artists also painted birds, animals and plants, such as bamboo or lotus. Sometimes just a few brush strokes were used to capture the spirit of the subject. Chinese writing in the form of a poem often played an important part in many pictures. Chinese artists also produced woodcuts, which are prints made from a carved wooden block. Traditionally these were not valued as much as the paintings, but many beautiful woodcuts were produced during the reign of the Ming dynasty (1368–1644).

SYMBOLS OF WISDOM
To the Chinese, the dragon embodied wisdom, strength and goodness. This intricate ivory seal belonged to a Ming emperor and shows a dragon guarding the pearl of wisdom.

WINDOW ON THE PAST
A royal procession makes its way along a mountain range. This detail from a painting on silk is by the great master Li Sixun (AD651–716). Many Tang dynasty paintings show court life and royal processions, but they are far from dull. They provide a colourful glimpse of life in China at that time. This picture shows what people wore and how they travelled.

MAKE PAPER CUT-OUTS
You will need: A4-sized coloured paper, pencil, ruler, scissors.

1 Take a piece of coloured paper and lay it flat on a hard surface. Fold it exactly in half widthways. Make a firm crease along the fold, as shown above.

2 Draw a Chinese-style design on the paper. Make sure all the shapes meet up at the fold. Make a tracing of your design so you can use it again.

3 Keeping the card folded, cut out shapes. Make sure you don't cut along the folded edge. Cut away areas you want to discard in between the shapes.

PAINTING NATURE

Morning mist hangs over a mountain backdop. This detail from a masterpiece by Qiu Ying (1494–1552) is inspired by the forests and mountain landscapes of his homeland. Artists such as Qiu Ying were successful and well paid.

AT FULL GALLOP

Chinese artists greatly admired horses and loved to try to capture their strength and movement in paintings. This lively wall painting was found in a Han dynasty tomb.

ART IN PORCELAIN

China's craft workers and designers were also great artists. This blue-and-white porcelain wine jar was made in the 1600s in the form of a mandarin duck and drake. Its hand-painted details would have taken many long hours of work to complete. Blue-and-white porcelain was very popular during the Ming dynasty.

SPRINGTIME ON PAPER

A watercolour painting from the 1800s shows peach blossom just as it comes into flower. It is painted in a very realistic, fresh and simple style. This approach is a common characteristic of much Chinese art.

4 Now open up your design. Be careful not to tear it. To add details to the figures, fold the paper again. Mark the details to be cut along the crease.

5 Using a pair of scissors, carefully cut out the detail along the crease. The cut-out detail will be matched perfectly on the other side of the figure.

Carefully open up your finished cut-out. Display the design by sticking it to a window, so that light shines through. In China, paper cut-outs are traditionally used to bring luck and good fortune.

The Written Word

THE CHINESE LANGUAGE is written with symbols called characters, which stand for sounds and words. They have changed and developed over the ages. A dictionary published in 1716 lists over 40,000 of them. Each character was written by hand with a brush, using 11 basic brush strokes. The painting of these beautiful characters is called calligraphy, and was always seen as a form of art.

The Chinese began using woodblocks for printing in about 1600BC. Before that, books had often been handwritten on bamboo strips. Ancient Chinese writers produced all sorts of practical handbooks and encyclopedias. Poetry first developed about 3,000 years ago. It was the Chinese who invented paper, nearly 2,000 years ago. Cloth or bark was shredded, pulped and dried on frames. Movable type was invented in the 1040s. During the 1500s popular folk tales such as *The Water Margin* were published, and in the 1700s the writer Cao Xuequin produced China's greatest novel, *A Dream of Red Mansions.*

MAGICAL MESSAGES
The earliest surviving Chinese script appears on animal bones. They were used for telling fortunes in about 1200BC. The script was made up of small pictures representing objects or ideas. Modern Chinese script is made up of patterns of lines.

ART OF CALLIGRAPHY
This text was handwritten during the Tang dynasty (AD618–906). Traditional Chinese writing reads down from right to left, starting in the top right-hand corner.

MAKE PRINTING BLOCKS

You will need: white paper, pencil, paint, soft Chinese brush or thin paintbrush, water pot, tracing paper, board, self-hardening clay (15 x 20cm/ 6 x 8in and 2.5cm/1in thick), modelling tool, wood glue, block printing ink, damp rag.

1 Copy or trace the characters from the reversed image block (see opposite). Start off with a pencil outline, then fill in with paint. Leave to dry.

2 Copy the design on to tracing paper. Turn the paper over. Place it on the clay. Scribble on the clean side of the paper to leave a mirror image in the clay.

3 Use a modelling tool to carve out characters. Cut away clay all around characters to make a relief (raised pattern). Smooth the clay base with your fingertips.

THE BEST WAY TO WRITE

A calligrapher of the 1840s begins to write, surrounded by his assistants. The brush must be held upright for the writing of Chinese characters. The wrist is never rested on the table. Many years of practice and study are necessary to become a good calligrapher.

THE PRINTED PAGE

The Buddhist scripture called the *Diamond Sutra* (*shown right*) is probably the oldest surviving printed book in the world. It includes both text and pictures. The book was printed from a woodblock on 11 May AD868 and was intended to be distributed at no cost to the public.

INKS AND COLOURS

Watercolours and inks were based on plant and mineral pigments in reds, browns, blues, greens and yellows. Black ink was made from carbon, obtained from soot. This was mixed with glue to form a solid block. The ink block would be wetted during use. Brushes were made from animal hair fitted into bamboo handles.

Chinese brushes

reversed image

actual image

Moon Ruler

Mouth Sun

Block rubbings of characters were an early form of printing.

4 When the relief has dried, paint the clay block with wood glue. Leave it to dry thoroughly. When dry, the glue seals and protects the pattern.

5 Now paint the design. Apply a thick layer of printing ink to the raised parts of the clay with a Chinese brush or a soft paintbrush.

6 Lay a thin piece of white paper over the inked block. Use a dry brush to press the paper into the ink, so that the paper takes up the design.

7 Lift up the paper to reveal your design. Look after your printing block by cleaning it with a damp rag. You can then use it again and again.

Musicians and Performers

THE EARLIEST CHINESE POETRY was sung rather than spoken. *Shijing* (the Book of Songs) dates back over 3,000 years and includes the words to hymns and folk songs. For most of China's history, musicians were employed in rich households. Orchestras played drums, gongs, pan pipes, racks of bronze bells, fiddles and other stringed instruments. Music was considered an important part of life, and models of musicians were often put in tombs to provide entertainment in the afterlife.

Musicians were frequently accompanied by acrobats, jugglers and magicians. Such acts were as popular in the markets and streets of the town as in the courtyards of nobles. Storytelling and puppet shows were equally well loved. Plays and opera became hugely popular in the 1200s, with tales of murder, intrigue, heroism and love acted out to music. Most of the female roles would be played by men.

THE COURT DANCER
Arching her right arm upwards, an elegant dancer performs at the royal court. The model's flowing dress belongs to the fashions of the Tang dynasty (AD618–906).

PUTTING ON A PUPPET SHOW
Children put on a show with marionettes (puppets moved by strings) in the 1600s. Drumming was used to provide musical accompaniment, just like in a professional play of the period.

MAKE A MASK
You will need: tape measure, large block of self-hardening clay, board, modelling tool, petroleum jelly, newspaper, wood glue and brush, scissors, thick cardboard, masking tape, 2 large white beads, paintbrush, paints (grey, cream, terracotta and yellow), water pot, needle, black wool, string.

1 Measure the width and length of your face with a tape measure. Make a clay mould. Carve out the eyes and attach a clay nose to the mask.

2 Paint front of mask with petroleum jelly. Apply 4–6 layers of papier mâché. This is made by soaking torn newspaper in water and glue. Leave to dry.

3 Remove mask from the clay mould. Cut a 2.5cm/1in-wide strip of card long enough to fit around your face. Bend it into a circle, and tape to the mask.

MUSIC IN THE GARDEN

Musicians in the 1800s play *qins* (lutes) and *sheng* (flutes) in a garden setting. The music tried to reflect nature's harmony. It was intended to make the listener feel peaceful and spiritual.

CHINESE OPERA

These stars of the Chinese opera are performing in the 1700s. Well-known folk tales were acted out to the dramatic sound of crashing cymbals and high-pitched singing. Elaborate make-up and fancy costumes made it clear to the audience whether the actor was playing a hero or a villain, a princess or a demon.

Elaborate masks like these were worn to great effect in Chinese opera. When your mask is finished, you can wear it to scare your friends!

SOUND THE DRUMS!

The cavalcade that followed an important government official or general might have included mounted drummers or trumpeters. These figures of musicians on horseback were found in the tomb of a high-ranking official from the Tang dynasty.

4 Cut two pointed ear shapes from card. Fold card at the edge to make flaps. Cut out and glue on small, decorative pieces of card. Glue ears to the mask.

5 Glue on two large white beads for the eyes. Cut out more small pieces of card. Glue these on above the eyes. Add another piece of card for lips.

6 Paint the mask with the grey base paint first. Leave to dry. Then add details using the brighter paints. When dry, varnish with wood glue.

7 Use a needle to thread black wool through for the beard, taping it to the back of the mask. Thread string through the sides behind the ears for tying it on.

Games and Pastimes

FROM EARLY IN CHINA'S history, kings and nobles loved to go hunting for pleasure. Horses and chariots were used to hunt deer and wild boar. Dogs and even cheetahs were trained to chase the prey. Spears, bows and arrows were then used to kill it. Falconry (using birds of prey to hunt animals) was commonplace by about 2000BC.

In the Ming and Qing dynasties ancient spiritual disciplines used by Daoist monks were brought together with the battle training used by warriors. These martial arts (*wu shu*) were intended to train both mind and body. They came to include the body movements known as tai chi (*taijiquan*), sword play (*jianwu*) and the extreme combat known as kung fu (*gongfu*).

Archery was a popular sport in imperial China. The Chinese also loved gambling, and may have invented the first card games over 2,000 years ago.

PEACE THROUGH MOVEMENT
A student of tai chi practises his art. The Chinese first developed the system of exercises known as tai chi more than 2,000 years ago. The techniques of tai chi were designed to help relax the human body and concentrate the mind.

CHINESE CHESS
The traditional Chinese game of *xiang qi* is similar to western chess. One army battles against another, with round discs used as playing pieces. To tell the discs apart, each is marked with a name.

pieces

xiang qi board

MAKE A KITE

You will need: 30cm/12in wooden skewers (x 12), ruler, scissors, glue and brush, plastic insulating tape, A1-size paper, pencil, paint (blue, red, yellow, black and pink), paintbrush, water pot, string, piece of wooden dowel, small metal ring.

1 Make a 40 x 30cm/16 x 12in rectangle by joining some of the sticks. Overlap the sticks for strength, then glue and tape together. Add a centre rod.

2 Make another rectangle, 15 x 40cm/6 x 16in. Overlay the second rectangle on top of the first. Tape the rectangles together, as shown above.

3 Place the frame on to the sheet of paper. Draw a 2.5cm/1in border around the outside of the frame. Add curves around the end of the centre rod.

BAMBOO BETTING

Gamblers place bets in a game of *liu po*. Bamboo sticks were thrown like dice to decide how far the counters on the board should move. Gambling was a widespread pastime during the Han dynasty. People would bet large sums of money on the outcome of card games, horse races and cock fights.

POLO PONIES

These women from the Tang dynasty are playing a fast and furious game of polo. They are probably noblewomen from the Emperor's royal court. The sport of polo was originally played in India and central Asia. It was invented as a training game to improve the riding skills of soldiers in cavalry units.

ALL-IN WRESTLING

This bronze figure of two wrestling muscle men was made in about 300BC. Wrestling was a very popular entertainment and sport in imperial China. It continues to be an attraction at country fairs and festivals.

Chinese children today still play with home-made paper kites. Kites were invented in China in about 400BC.

4 Cut out the kite shape from the paper. Using a pencil, draw the details of a dragon design on the paper. Paint in your design and leave to dry.

5 Cut a triangular piece of paper to hang from the end of your kite as a tail. Fold the tail over the rod at the bottom of the kite. Tape into position.

6 Carefully tape and glue your design on to the frame. Fold over the border that you allowed for when cutting out the paper. Tape to back of paper, as shown.

7 Wrap 10m/30ft of string around dowel. Tie other end to ring. Pass two pieces of string through kite from the back. Tie to centre rod. Tie other ends to ring.

Travel by Land

THE CHINESE EMPIRE was linked by a network of roads used only by the army, officials and royal messengers. A special carriageway was reserved for the emperor himself. Ordinary people travelled along dusty or muddy routes and tracks.

China's mountainous landscape and large number of rivers meant that Chinese engineers became expert at bridge-building. Suspension bridges made of rope and bamboo were being used from about AD1 onwards. A bridge suspended from iron chains crossed the Chang Jiang (Yangzi River) as early as AD580. A stone arch bridge built in about AD615 still stands today at Zhouxian in Hebei province. Most people travelled by foot and porters often had to carry great loads on their backs. They also carried wealthy people from place to place on litters (chairs).

China's small native ponies were interbred with larger, stronger horses from central Asia sometime after 100BC. This provided fast, powerful mounts that were suitable for messengers and officials, and they were also capable of pulling chariots and carriages. Mules and camels were widely used along the trade routes of the north, while shaggy yaks carried loads in the high mountains of the Himalayas. Carts were usually hauled along by oxen.

HEADING OUT WEST
Chinese horsemen escort the camels of a caravan (trading expedition). The traders are about to set out along the Silk Road. This trading route ran all the way from Chang'an (Xian) in China right through to Europe and the lands of the Mediterranean.

RIDING ON HORSEBACK
A Chinese nobleman from about 2,000 years ago reins in his elegant horse. Breaking in the horse would have been difficult, as the rider has no stirrups and could easily be unseated. Metal stirrups were in general use in China by AD302. They provided more stability and helped to improve the rider's control of the horse.

CARRIED BY HAND

A lazy landowner of the Qing dynasty travels around his estates. He is carried along in a litter, a platform supported by the shoulders of his tired, long-suffering servants. An umbrella shades the landowner from the heat of the summer sun.

CAMEL POWER

Bactrian (two-humped) camels were originally bred in central Asia. They could endure the extremes of heat and cold of the region, and travel for long distances without water. This toughness made them ideal for transporting goods along the Silk Road.

HAN CARRIAGE

During the Han period, three-horse carriages were used by the imperial family only. This carving from a tomb brick is probably of a messenger carrying an important order from the emperor.

TRAVELLING IN STYLE

During the Han dynasty, government officials travelled in stylish horse-drawn carriages. This picture is taken from a decorative brick found in a Han tomb. After larger, stronger breeds of horses were introduced into China from central Asia, the horse became a status symbol for the rich and powerful. Such horses were considered to be celestial (heavenly).

Junks and Sampans

FROM EARLY IN CHINA'S history, its rivers, lakes and man-made canals were the country's main highways. Fishermen propelled small wooden boats across the water with a single oar or pole at the stern. These small boats were often roofed with mats, like the sampans (which means 'three planks' in Chinese) still seen today. Large wooden sailing ships, which we call junks, sailed the open ocean. They were either keeled or flat-bottomed, with a high stern and square bows. Their sails were made of matting stiffened with strips of bamboo. By the AD800s, Chinese shipbuilders had built the first ships with several masts and proper rudders.

In the 1400s, admirals Zheng He and Wang Jinghong led seven sea expeditions that visited South-east Asia, India, Arabia and East Africa. The flagship of their 300-strong naval fleet was over five times the size of the largest European ships of the time.

IN FULL SAIL
Junks were a type of sailing vessel used by merchants in the East and South China seas. They were also used by pirates. The China seas could be blue and peaceful, but they were often whipped into a fury by typhoons (tropical storms).

RIVER TRAFFIC
All sorts of small trading boats were sailed or rowed along China's rivers in the 1850s. River travel was often difficult and could be dangerous. Floods were common along the Huang He (Yellow River), which often changed course. The upper parts of China's longest river, the Chang Jiang (Yangzi River), were rocky and had powerful currents.

MAKE A SAMPAN

You will need: ruler, pencil, thick and thin card, scissors, glue and brush, masking tape, 6 wooden skewers, string, thin yellow paper, paint (black, dark brown), paintbrush, water pot.

39cm/15½in
1cm/½in
Runner A (x 2)

33.5cm/13¼in
Side B (x 2)   5cm/2in
15cm/6in

Base C (x 2)   7cm/2¾in   Base D
15cm/6in   18cm/7in

Floor E   7cm/2¾in   4cm/1½in   Floor F (x 2)
10cm/4in   7cm/2¾in   Edge G (x 2)   1cm/½in
6.5cm/2¼in

Cut pieces B, C, D and G from thick card.
Cut pieces A, E, and F from thin card.

1 Glue base pieces C and D to side B, as shown. Hold the pieces with masking tape while the glue dries. When dry, remove the masking tape.

2 Glue remaining side B to the boat. Stick runner A pieces to top of the sides. Make sure the ends jut out 2.5cm/1in at the front and back of the boat.

expedition routes

THE VOYAGES OF ZHENG HE

Chinese admirals Zheng He and Wang Jinghong carried out seven fantastic voyages of exploration between 1405 and 1433. This map shows how far and wide they travelled on these expeditions. Their impressive fleets included over 60 ships crewed by about 27,000 seamen, officers and interpreters. The biggest of their vessels was 147m/482ft long and 60m/197ft wide.

THE FISHING TRIP

A fisherman poles his boat across the river in the 1500s. The bird shown in the picture is a tamed cormorant, used for catching the fish. The cormorant was normally attached to a line, with a ring around its neck to prevent it from swallowing the fish.

FISHERMEN'S FEASTS

Seas, lakes and rivers were an important food source in imperial China. Drying fish was often the only way to preserve it in the days before refrigeration. Dried fish made strong-tasting sauces and soups. Popular shellfish included crabs, shrimp and squid.

dried fish

dried squid

To add the finishing touch to your sampan, make a boatman and oar to propel the vessel through the waterways.

3 Glue floor E to centre of base. Add floor F pieces to the ends of the base, as shown. Stick edge G pieces in between the ends of the runners.

4 Bend two skewers into 10cm/ 4in-high arches. Cut two skewers into five 10cm/4in struts. Glue and tie two struts to sides of the arches and one to the top.

5 Repeat step 4 to make a second roof. To make roof matting, cut thin yellow paper into 1 x 10cm/½ x 4in strips. Fold in half and stick to roofs.

6 Paint boat and roofs. Allow to dry. Glue the matting strips to the roofs, as shown. When the glue is dry, place roofs inside the boat.

Soldiers and Weapons

IN CHINA'S EARLY HISTORY, bitter warfare between local rulers devastated the countryside with an appalling cost in human lives. Battle tactics and campaigns were discussed in *The Art of War* by Master Sun, who lived in the 500s BC at around the same time as the thinker Kong Fuzi (Confucius). This was the first book of its kind and its ideas are still studied today. After the empire was united in 221BC, rulers still needed large armies to stay in power and to guard against invasion.

The first Chinese armies fought with horse-drawn chariots and bronze weapons. Later, battles were fought with iron weapons, horsemen and hundreds of thousands of footsoldiers. Armour was made of metal, lacquered leather or padded quilting. Weapons included bows and arrows, powerful crossbows, swords and halberds (long blades on poles). As the empire grew, the Han Chinese came into conflict with the many peoples whose lands now lay in China.

PRECIOUS SPEAR
This spearhead is over 3,200 years old. It was made from the precious stone jade set in bronze and turquoise. The spear was intended for ceremonial use, as it was far too precious to be used in combat.

SOLDIER ON HORSEBACK
A Tang dynasty warrior sits astride his horse, ready for battle. His horse is also ready to fight, covered by a protective jacket. The warrior's feet are supported by stirrups. These were useful in combat, as they allowed a soldier to remain steady in the saddle as he fought.

MAKE CHINESE ARMOUR

You will need: 150 x 70cm/ 1.5yd x 28in piece of felt fabric, scissors, large sewing needle, string, silver card, ruler, pencil, tape, split pins, silver paint, paintbrush, water pot, thick card, glue and brush.

1 Fold felt fabric in half. Cut a semicircle along the fold to make a neck hole. Put garment on. Trim so it just reaches your hips and covers your shoulders.

2 Use scissors to make two holes either side of the waist. Pass string through holes. Secure as shown. The string will be used to tie the garment to your waist.

3 Cut 70 squares (5 x 5cm/ 2 x 2in) out of silver card. Lay a row of overlapping squares face down at the top of the fabric. Tape the rows together.

FIGHTING ON THE GREAT WALL

In 1884–85, heavily armed French soldiers engaged in battle with the Chinese. The empire was in decline by the 1880s, and its outdated tactics were no match for the superior might of the French forces.

BATTLING HAN

This battered-looking helmet would once have protected a Han soldier's head from crossbow bolts, sword blows and arrows. Young men were conscripted into the Chinese army and had to serve as soldiers for at least two years. During this time they received no payment. However, they were supplied with food, weapons and armour.

FRONTIER GUARD

A battle-hardened soldier keeps guard with his shield and spear. A warrior like this would have kept watch over the precious Silk Road in a distant outpost of the Chinese empire. This model dates from the reign of the Tang emperor Taizong (AD626–649).

To put on your armour, pull the undergarment over your head. Ask a friend to help with the waist ties. Make holes in the shoulder pads and tie on with string.

4 Make enough rows to cover fabric. Trim card to fit at the neck. Tape rows together. Take armour off fabric and turn over. Attach split pins at all corners.

5 Place armour over fabric. Push split pins through top and bottom corners of armour. Pass pins through fabric and fasten. Paint split pins silver.

6 Cut shoulder pads out of thick card. Cut out 5cm/2in squares of silver card to cover pads. Glue to card. Push split pins through. Paint pins silver.

Festivals and Customs

THE CHINESE FESTIVAL best known around the world today is the New Year or Spring Festival. Its date varies according to the traditional Chinese calendar, which is based on the phases of the moon. The festival is marked by dancers carrying a long dragon through the streets, accompanied by loud, crackling firecrackers to scare away evil spirits. The festival has been celebrated for over 2,000 years and has always been a time for family feasts and village carnivals. The doorways of buildings are traditionally decorated with hand-written poetry on strips of red paper to bring luck and good fortune for the coming year.

Soon after New Year, sweet dumplings made of rice flour are prepared for the Lantern Festival. Paper lanterns are hung out to mirror the first full moon of the year. This festival began during the Tang dynasty (AD618–906). In the eighth month of the year, the autumn full moon is marked by the eating of special moon cakes. Chinese festivals are linked to agricultural seasons. They include celebrations of sowing and harvest, dances, horse races and the eating of specially prepared foods.

DANCING ANIMALS
Chinese New Year parades are often headed by a lion *(shown above)* or dragon. These are carried by dancers accompanied by crashing cymbals.
The first month of the Chinese calendar begins on the first full moon between 21 January and 19 February.

HORSE RACING
The Mongols, who invaded China in the 1200s, brought with them their love of horses and superb riding skills. Today, children as young as three years old take part in horse-racing festivals in northern China and Mongolia. Archery and wrestling competitions are also regularly held.

MAKE A LANTERN

You will need: thick cardboard, pencil, ruler, scissors, pair of compasses, glue and brush, red tissue paper, blue paint, paintbrush, water pot, thin blue and yellow card, wire, tape, bamboo stick, torch, fringing fabric.

25cm/10in

Frame
(x 4)

18cm/7in

1cm/½in
2.5cm/1in

18cm/7in

Side
(x 4)

16cm/6¼in

End
(x 2)

18cm/7in

Using the measurements above, draw the 10 pieces on to thick card (pieces not drawn to scale). Cut out pieces with scissors.

1 Using a pair of compasses, draw an 8cm/3¼in-diameter circle in the middle of one of the end pieces. Cut out. Glue on the four sides, as shown.

2 Glue together the frame pieces. Then glue the end pieces on to the frame. When dry, cover frame with red tissue paper. Glue one side at a time.

DRAGON BOATS

In the fifth month of the Chinese year, races are held in the Dragon Boat festival. This is in memory of a famous statesman called Qu Yuan, who drowned himself in 278BC when his advice to his ruler was ignored. Rice dumplings are eaten at the Dragon Boat festival every year in his memory.

CHINESE LANTERNS

Elaborate paper lanterns brighten up a wedding in the 1800s during the Qing dynasty. Lanterns were also strung up or paraded on poles at other private celebrations and during Chinese festivals.

3 Paint the top of lantern blue. Cut borders out of blue card. Glue to top and bottom of frame. Stick a thin strip of yellow card to bottom border.

4 Make two small holes opposite each other at the top of the lantern. Pass the ends of a loop of wire through each. Bend and tape ends.

5 Make a hook from thick card. Split the end opposite hook. Glue and wrap around bamboo stick. Hang lantern by wire loop from hook.

Light up your lantern by placing a small torch inside it. Decorate with a fringe. Now you can join in Chinese celebrations!

Glossary

A

abacus A wooden frame with beads on rods, used for calculating.

acupuncture The treatment of the body with fine needles to relieve pain or cure illness.

alloy A substance made by mixing two or more different metals.

ancestor An individual from whom one is descended, such as a great, great-grandfather.

Anno Domini (AD) A system used to calculate dates after the supposed year of Christ's birth. Anno Domini dates in this book are prefixed AD up to the year 1000 (e.g. AD521). After 1000, no prefixes are used (e.g. 1912).

archaeologist A person who studies ancient ruins and remains.

astronomy The scientific study of stars, planets and other heavenly bodies. In ancient times it was often mixed up with astrology, the belief that heavenly bodies shape our lives.

B

banquet A rich, elaborate feast served with great ceremony.

barter To trade by exchanging goods rather than by paying money.

Before Christ (BC) A system used to calculate dates before the supposed year of Christ's birth. Dates are calculated in reverse (e.g. 200BC is longer ago than 1BC). Before Christ dates are followed by the letters BC (e.g. 455BC).

bellows A mechanism for pumping air into a fire or furnace.

Buddhism The religious teachings of the Buddha, which first came to China from India.

C

character One of the symbols used in Chinese script.

civilization A society that makes advances in law, government, the arts and technology.

civil servant Official who carries out government administration.

Confucianism The Western name for the teachings of the philosopher Kong Fuzi (Confucius), which call for social order and respect for one's family and ancestors.

cormorant A coastal and river bird that can be trained to catch fish.

crossbow A mechanical bow that fires small arrows called bolts.

D

Daoism A Chinese philosophy based on contemplation of the natural world. It later became a religion with a belief in magic.

derrick The tower-like frame that supports drilling equipment.

dynasty A period of rule by emperors of the same royal family. The most important dynasties in the history of the Chinese empire are listed below:

XIA (c.2100BC–c.1600BC)
SHANG (c.1600BC–1122BC)
ZHOU (1122BC–221BC)
 WESTERN ZHOU (1122BC-771BC)
 EASTERN ZHOU (771BC–221BC)
QIN (221BC–206BC)
HAN (206BC–AD220)
THREE KINGDOMS PERIOD (AD220–280)
JIN (AD265–420)
NORTHERN AND SOUTHERN DYNASTIES (AD420–581)
SUI (AD581–618)
TANG (AD618–906)
FIVE KINGDOMS AND TEN DYNASTIES PERIOD (AD906–960)
SONG (AD960–1279)
YUAN (1279–1368)
MING (1368–1644)
QING (1644–1912)

E

escapement A type of ratchet used in clockwork timing mechanisms.

F

filament A fine strand of fibre.

Forbidden City The royal palace in Beijing, made up of hundreds of buildings set inside high walls.

H

harmony A pleasing sense of order, based on peace and balance.

hemp A fibrous plant, often used to make coarse textiles and clothes.

I

imperial Relating to the rule of an emperor or empress.

Islam The Muslim faith, which proclaims that there is only one God and that his messenger is the prophet Muhammad.

J

jade Either of two hard, precious minerals called jadeite and nephrite. Jade is white or green in colour.

joinery Skilled woodworking needed for making fine furniture.

junk A traditional Chinese sailing ship with square sails.

K

kaolin A fine white clay used in porcelain and paper making.

kitchen god A god whose picture was kept in Chinese kitchens.

L

lacquer A thick, coloured varnish used to coat wood, metal or leather.

lodestone A type of magnetic iron ore, also called magnetite.

loom A frame or machine used for weaving cloth.

lotus A type of water lily.

lychee A soft Chinese fruit.

M

magistrate An imperial officer of justice, similar to a local judge.

martial arts Physical exercises that are often based upon combat, such as swordplay and kung fu. Chinese martial arts bring together spiritual and physical disciplines.

merchant A person who buys and sells goods for a profit.

millet A type of grain crop.

minting The process by which new coins are produced.

mother-of-pearl A hard, shiny substance found in shells, also known as nacre. It was often used in jewellery inlays by skilled Chinese craft workers.

moxibustion The transfer of heat to the body from burning herbs.

mung beans The seeds of the Asian mung plant. Often used as a source of bean sprouts.

myth Any ancient tale or legend that describes gods, spirits or fantastic creatures.

P

pagoda A high, multi-storey tower found in eastern and southern Asia. Pagodas were often used as libraries or places of religious worship.

peasant A poor country dweller.

pigment Any material used to provide colour for paint or ink.

pinyin The official romanized spelling of the Chinese language, used for terms and place names in this book. In pinyin, the letter q is pronounced as *ch*.

porcelain The finest quality of pottery. It was made with kaolin and baked at a high temperature.

province Part of the empire marked off for administrative purposes.

R

ritual An often repeated series of solemn actions, normally carried out for a religious purpose.

S

sampan A small wooden boat with a cabin made of matting.

seismoscope An instrument that reacts to earthquakes and tremors.

sericulture The production of silk.

Silk Road The overland trading route that, in ancient times, stretched from northern China through Asia to Europe.

silkworm The larva (caterpillar) of a silkmoth. It produces silken threads that it spins into a cocoon.

smelt To extract a metal from its ore by heating it in a furnace.

suspension bridge A bridge in which the roadway is suspended (hung) from towers.

T

temple A building used for worship or rituals. Such buildings were often specially designed for this purpose.

terracotta A composition of baked clay and sand used to make statues, figurines and pottery.

textile Any cloth that has been woven, such as silk or cotton.

threshing To beat or thrash out grain from the corn.

tomb A vault in which dead bodies are placed. In imperial China, the tombs of emperors and noblemen were often filled with beautiful objects of great value.

W

ward A walled district found in the cities of imperial China.

warlord A man who keeps a private army and controls a large region of the country by force.

winnow To sift the grain from the chaff (husks) of the corn.

wisteria A Chinese climbing shrub with blue flowers.

X

xianq qi A traditional Chinese board game, similar to the Western game of chess.

Y

yak A long-haired ox, used in Tibet as a beast of burden.

yin and yang The Daoist belief in two life forces that must be balanced to achieve harmony. Ying is negative, feminine and dark, while yang is positive, masculine and light.

Index